The Sexualization of America's Kids

The Sexualization of America's Kids

And How to Stop It

J.E. WRIGHT

iUniverse, Inc.
Bloomington

The Sexualization of America's Kids
And How to Stop It

iUniverse books may be ordered through booksellers or by contacting:

iUniverse
1663 Liberty Drive
Bloomington, IN 47403
www.iuniverse.com
1-800-Authors (1-800-288-4677)

ISBN: 978-1-4620-0846-9 (sc)
ISBN: 978-1-4620-0847-6 (ebk)

Printed in the United States of America

iUniverse rev. date: 3/19/2011

Contents

Introduction

When I was growing up, sex was simply not talked about in direct ways. Comments were made like, "Oh, you must come from a Catholic family," or "Don't be staring at the girls," but no one told me what everyone was referring to. I pieced together bits of sexual information throughout my teenage years, and as a result I was extremely uncomfortable talking to girls to whom I was attracted. Currently, sex is still not talked about in direct ways; however, our media has exploded with sexualized messages and disrespectful displays of both sexes. To even keep up with what our growing kids were exposed to, my wife and I had to talk about direct sexual education issues in caring ways with our kids several times a week. These talks took the form of comfortably using the correct words for all body parts when they were young. We also talked about the special hugs people have with each other when they are in love, and having respectful picture books available when they were in grade school, and about emotionally healthy and unhealthy kinds of touch. We added more intimate picture books that were available when they were teenagers. The closeness and maturity these personal talks created with our kids was a joy to experience and watch as they grew up.

In my 22 years as a therapist, I have not witnessed anything as consistently destructive to our children and teenagers as the way sexuality is dealt with in our society. The effects of drugs, violence, and divorce are certainly factors, but they are openly talked about and numerous programs continue to be established. Sex is kept under the table, and its continual, yet subtle effect is delaying, and in many cases, eroding our kids' emotional development. This "silence-on-sex" phenomenon is partly due to men not wanting to talk about it because it threatens their power base by equalizing the sexes. Too many men want women to take a "back seat" and just agree with their ideas and opinions, but it is primarily a problem of parents being too uncomfortable to dialogue. As a result, we have unconsciously relegated the on-going sexuality education of our children to the prevailing norms of the media and their peers. Although on the surface this has been easy for parents and fun for our kids, it has significantly hindered everyone's ability to talk respectfully about the opposite sex.

In many cases, our growing kids seem to know more about sex than we do. Although this may be true concerning the details of sex or current dating norms, our kids are missing something that only parents can give them: what a truly caring and giving relationship really feels like, and how respectful affection and touch fit into loving relationships. This type of caring respectfulness is something our kids will never learn from our sexualized media or movies, but rather through actual personal experience.

If our kids laugh and turn away or we feel embarrassed to the point of silence when sexuality topics arise, they are not learning or experiencing the respectful aspect of the opposite sex. The most noticeable fallout seen in children raised without respectful openness is the fear in their eyes when sexual topics come up or their obsession of avoiding playing with the opposite sex. Although games like "boy germs or girl germs" may appear minor, it is early grooming for a separation of the sexes, rather than a working together attitude. A noticeable fallout seen in teenagers is their inability to sustain open, caring, and on-going friendships with the opposite sex. In my practice, many teenage girls complain, "I can't just be friends with guys because they always want to go out or forget it." Many of the teenage boys complain, "I always have to be on with girls and making them laugh, otherwise they don't like you."

These kids have been unconsciously raised to play the boyfriend or girlfriend game, and without frequent parental input and equal sex opportunities from a young age these teenagers are like ships passing in the night. Both sexes want to be connected as friends without all of the romantic, sexual trappings, but they have no knowledge or experience of how to do it. It is this mis-education of our children and teenagers that leads far too many of them into inappropriate or naive, yet hurtful behavior toward the opposite sex.

Regarding sexuality, there are two ways to protect and nurture our children and teenagers. The first one is to pass new laws and develop mandatory guidelines for our media to follow. The second is to educate and demonstrate to our children and teenagers caring and respectful sexuality, not only in our words, but also in our actions. This book focuses on the second way.

There has been much work and significant gains in the first area; however, it's taking too long and we are losing precious teaching time for our children and teenagers. In this book I will concentrate on the changes that parents and families can actually make on their own: concrete actions that create positive results. It is an opposite approach than the one we take with the media. In dealing with the media we have to develop mandatory guidelines. In my approach with families, I recommend completely opening up the whole area of sexuality in a caring, respectful, and appropriate way. I believe, and have seen that these recommendations have an immediate and positive effect on children and teenagers. Developmentally, it is the only way children can learn.

Initially, this new approach will be uncomfortable and challenging for most parents and adults. It may even seem like too much. However, when compared to the high frequency of the self-centered, negatively sexualized messages our children and teenagers receive daily through different media forms, it is truly the only sensible alternative for raising healthy kids. I believe what the great educator John Holt once said, "The only preparation for bad is good."

This book is based on the premise that caring and respectful openness toward sexuality, from a young age, is the optimal path to maturity and the best form of countering our media today. It is also based on the premise that intimate sexual touch is only meaningful and sound within a caring, committed relationship. The caring feelings that slowly grow within a committed relationship are what give true meaning and appropriateness to all touch and affection.

Any personal touch or sexual contact outside of a caring and committed relationship is similar to buying gifts to win friends, or a new stepparent moving in and taking charge of parenting a new spouse's children. An established relationship is not yet present, and therefore interactions become tense and hollow. Without the necessary time needed to build real trust and feelings for another, a relationship exists merely on the surface and quickly deteriorates into anger and apathy.

This book suggests a new and completely open and caring approach to teaching sexuality and its appropriate place within family and human relationships. It will instill in our children and teenagers the knowledge and maturity to navigate through the self-centeredness and shallowness of the media's presentations of sexuality and relationships. They will also become naturally skilled at discerning the difference between affection and sexual intimacy that is appropriate and real or superficial and selfish.

The recommendations for change are sometimes uncomfortable and the methods need practice. They are meant to empower parents and to nurture children and teenagers beyond the negative impact of our media and to create a strong personality core for their passage into adulthood. A concerted effort by parents and adults with this new approach is our kids' best chance for maturity because they will not learn it completely and respectfully from peers or the media.

Prelude

Jacob (10)

A talkative, energetic boy, Jacob, was referred to me by his school because he had made inappropriate sexual comments to the girls in his class. He was in the fourth grade and doing well academically. His mother reluctantly brought Jacob to my counseling office and stated that his father couldn't make the appointment.

"Yeah, he's home watching TV," Jacob added while examining a game in my office. "Can we play this while we talk?" While I asked questions, Jacob, his mother, and I played a board game.

"I don't know why they told me to bring him to counseling," his mother said. "Every boy acts like that once in a while."

"Yeah, even Dad, right Mom?" Jacob appeared happy as he talked and moved ahead of his mother and me on the board game.

I asked her to explain further. "Oh, you know, saying sweet comments to the girls to get their attention."

"Like what?" I asked.

She turned to her son, "Tell him, Jacob."

"Oh, it's nothing. Just things like 'hey baby, wanna get together tonight?'" He giggled to himself and added, "One time I told this girl she was hot."

"Another time," his mother said, "in the lunchroom, he was staring at a girl and when she looked at him he said, 'Yeah, I love ya.'"

"Ahh, that was funny," Jacob said, giggling again, "I don't even know why she got so mad."

"You mean scared," his mother interjected.

"Whatever," Jacob retorted.

After a minute of silence, Jacob's mother explained that he had three older brothers and one older sister. Her other sons were busy with their own friends, but her daughter usually had time for Jacob.

"I like playing with Julie," he said. "She's nice to me."

"Yes, I know you get along with your sister and I know your brothers tease you a lot, but it's just between brothers."

"No it's not," Jacob said. "Their friends make fun of me, too!"

"Well, I do say something to his brothers once in a while," his mother said, then turning toward Jacob, "but you know you could play with your friends instead of trying to hang around your brothers."

"I don't have any friends," Jacob shouted. "No one plays with me except Julie."

Jacob's brothers were 17, 16, and 14. His sister was 13. His dad worked a rotating shift at a local factory, and his mom worked days. The kids were usually on their own after school until Mom got home and made dinner. Their evenings were spent at home.

"We relax by watching television," she stated. "It takes our minds off our jobs."

"Dad watches more TV than anybody," Jacob said.

"Well, Jacob," his mother chided, "sometimes he's got long hours and you know how hard he works."

"Yeah, I know," Jacob conceded.

After the board game, I had Mom wait while I spent some individual time with Jacob. He talked about having a hard time getting up for school. He never had homework and he hoped to join the Army when he got older. He also bragged about having girlfriends.

"I like talking to girls. They're so fine they blow my mind. That's a song, you know." He laughed and added, "I always have girlfriends to mess with." Then he looked around and asked more about the things in my office.

When answering my questions, he didn't seem to understand what was so unusual about the way he talked to girls. "Me and my brothers always talk like that." "How about your Dad?" I asked. He laughed and said, "He doesn't talk to anybody unless he's mad." Jacob played another game with me and talked about his favorite TV show, his favorite music, and more girlfriends. When I said our time was over, he asked, "Can you buy me a treat from the candy machine?"

I said, "Sure I could," and as we walked down the hallway to the machine, he held my hand.

1.) The Issue

A.) The Trick

How sex is dealt with inappropriately in our society

The stories vary from Jacob's, but the plot is the same. Kids in our communities are being groomed for sexually disrespectful and superficial behavior. Girls are raised to be pretty and display themselves and boys are raised to be aggressive and show off their accomplishments. These patterns can be normal if they remain a small part of our kids' lives; however, the importance of looking good has become an obsession in our society. Our kids are getting up every morning, knowing that what they wear and how they look has a profound effect on how they will be treated at school. The effect on girls is that it habitualizes them to ignore their opinions and true personalities for the sake of beauty. The effect on boys is that it teaches them to ignore their feelings for the sake of looking cool and in control. These patterns are creating kids who are focused on surface issues and can become one of the biggest aspects of their socialization. Although advertisers and entertainers invest their time and energies into maintaining this superficial focus, it is for the purpose of money, not out of concern for our kids. These surface patterns serve only those who pocket the profits. It has very little to do with care and concern for raising strong and independent-minded thinkers.

Some children and teenagers can bypass the daily hype to find self-confidence and belonging in more meaningful ways. These are the kids whose parents have shown them a different reality. They have experienced a daily, caring connection, on-going, respectful actions, and frequent verbal openness with their parents. These are the kids whose parents also allow them to occasionally play out what they see in the media, because to completely restrict a child's play away from media norms would give it more power. For example, allowing a 6-year-old girl to dress-up like a beauty pageant princess for Halloween. It's fun for her to act out and experiment with dressing-up because it gives her the experience through play which prepares her for real life. Another example is a parent who plays along with their teenager's wishes to be rich and popular in a conversation about their dreams. It's playful banter that keeps a teenager connected with their parent and feeling accepted for even their craziest wishes, and it's the connection with a parent that is important for our kid's mature development, not so much what is being played-out.

The safety these parents provide for their kids by allowing them to play out what they witness in our society is that it's not their only reality. After the playing is over, these parents include plenty of time for attending to and nurturing their kids' other emotional needs. This is done by listening and talking about all personal topics, demonstrating the art of compromise in relationships, holding kids accountable for respectful behavior by using consequences, being able to laugh at themselves and admit when they have made a mistake, and being affectionate. This is where kids learn and experience the deeper, more important aspects of life and relationships. However, because it requires much effort to pull away from the media's ways and parent more attentively, too often parents let down and acquiesce to the media's standards. Without consistent, parental involvement in calm and caring ways, our kids also succumb to the pervasiveness of the media and simply go along with its prevailing norms.

The trick is the seductive and sexually provocative way in which our media is presented. Its success depends on the lack of parental involvement in the important relationship areas of openness on personal topics, caring time spent together, and attentiveness to age-appropriate privileges and consequences. If we, as parents, are not living a different, open, and more caring life than what the media portrays, our kids are vulnerable to the media's tricks, and therefore can unconsciously fall into superficial and self-centered behaviors.

Visual Tricks

The media's provocativeness is usually shown in four areas of the human body to visually entice viewers: the face, breasts, buttocks, and legs. The majority of advertisers use female models; however, male models are also used. The images are packed with titillation by using coyish, serious, and innocent or victim-like faces. They hold attention by showing breasts or cleavage at various angles. They stimulate a sexual spark by showing legs and buttocks in unusual positions.

Jean Kilbourne, in her 1999 book, *Deadly Persuasions*, directly confronts and uncovers numerous manipulations of our mass media.[1] She outlines how women and girls are used as objects, and that advertising works because we are not fully aware of what it's doing to us. If we can learn to recognize advertising tricks by examining and talking about them, we can begin to resist its pull. I believe the same is true for sexuality. The more our kids understand and know about sex in caring ways, the less they will be influenced and tricked by our over-sexualized media.

Currently, the idea behind advertisers is to stay a step ahead of those watching in order to hold their attention and imprint their product image on as many human senses and emotions as possible. The manipulation is that they're evoking and playing with intimate human emotions to do it. Instead of using humor or cleverness, which is more light and general in their emotional impact, they primarily focus directly on individual sexual emotions. Although this is a smart marketing technique, it is used so frequently by the media that kids see nothing else. The world they experience through the media is filled with sexualized images, messages, and role models. When kids are raised in our society with constant sexualized flashes, they begin to see the world around them only for it's sexual content. This infiltration of sexual messages is so pervasive that it dulls our kids to the deeper meaning of sex and habitualizes them to a superficial language for such an intimate aspect of all of our lives.

---

1   Jean Kilbourne

In summary, the visual trick of the media is using intimate human images and emotions to promote an inanimate product. It works to sell their product, but its fallout lies in desensitizing our kids to an important and personal part of human intimacy. Desensitized kids do not know how to communicate respectfully on important sexual matters and struggle to make mature decisions within their romantic relationship. The media's trick is too quick and superficial for them to learn anything about real life personal topics, and its overuse pushes aside the opportunity for more personal and meaningful dialogue in relationships.

Feeling Tricks

Feeling tricks are a take-off from visual tricks. If visual tricks work by holding one's attention, then feeling tricks work by taking over and making viewers feel good. Whether it's about the possibility of being more attractive, sexy, or warmly identifying with the actors or models, the intent behind feeling tricks is to make the images last longer in our memories by evoking exciting or warm emotions.

Whenever we find ourselves smiling or warmly talking about what we just viewed, the feeling trick has worked. In movies, the feeling response is appropriate because one is identifying with a relationship situation. In advertising, the feeling response is primarily inappropriate or a trick because one is being subtly manipulated into having a feeling response to an image or product. Both are superficial and concrete; however, they are being pushed into a personal or inner aspect of our lives. Whenever our inner emotional lives are not reserved for relationship situations and feelings and inanimate product responses are allowed constant access, the numbing process is occurring. Humans simply cannot continually be bombarded with feeling responses to everything around them without becoming either numb or spread too thin. Our inner emotional responses maintain integrity and deepness only by reserving our personal energy for relationships.

Another part of feeling tricks is that advertisers don't really care what kind of feelings they elicit. As long as it's a feeling, they have successfully imprinted their product on the viewer. Whether it's anxious titillation from viewing models under eighteen years of age posing in sexually provocative positions, or being sexually sparked from viewing a loosely clad female in a coyish position or expression, it doesn't matter to the advertiser. They will utilize personal, out-of-relationship context images and private sexualized intimacy if it will evoke a feeling response and sell their product. It is this lack of concern that their presentation has on our kids, except for profit, which makes it an incredibly subtle manipulation and an offensive trick. Without appropriate concern and actions from adults, children and teenagers falter in discerning the difference between manipulated feelings and the two-way or mutual feelings present in personal relationships.

Sound Tricks

In order to enhance visual images and evoke feeling responses, advertisers use various sounds. These include music, singing, groans and other guttural noises, as well as magnified rhythm or bass. These background sounds exaggerate a mood and through their vibrations, they draw viewers in. The majority of these sounds are timed perfectly to match a woman's walk with the beat of a drum, an enlightened face with a pleasurable sigh, or a provocative pose with a distant scream.

Usually our eyesight is on overload when viewing a commercial, so we are not consciously aware of all of the sounds. However, if one closes their eyes and just listens to certain advertisements, the unusual mixture and hardness of the sounds becomes apparent. Without knowing what product is being advertised, it is rare that one would associate it with the dubbed-in sounds.

Again, advertisers have very little concern for the overall or long-term effects on our kids, as long as it works to sell their product. This approach to and use of our kids, is careless, degrading, and encourages self-centeredness. When our kids are constantly hit with these kinds of messages, it refines and grooms personal showiness, rather than true concern for others.

These three tricks—visual, feeling, and sound—are continually used by advertisers to discount our kids' individual differences, fool them into not thinking for themselves, and use them for their money, rather than addressing their intelligence.

Grooming

One of the biggest areas of influence in teenagers' lives is their friends. This is considered developmentally normal; however, parents also need to respectfully preserve their influence because a teenager's developing identity is still young. If parents back off too quickly when raising teenagers, peer influence takes over. In this case, teenagers have too much outside influence to incorporate before their identities are individually strong. Unformed, or not yet strong identities in teenagers make them extremely susceptible to peer influence. Friends, and teenagers in general, get most of their up-dates and styles from two sources: television and magazines.

The majority of programs and commercials teenagers view on television are focused on looking beautiful, acting cool, and learning how to get some of the spotlight. Many programs have occasional important life lessons, but the barrage of being more clever than another, the self-centered focus on looking good, and the incessant efforts at being in the spotlight tend to dominate them. Their lines are set up, the laughter is canned, and the scenes are artificially created. It's not real life, and it's not indicative of how real-life relationships work. Occasionally, these programs can be entertaining, but a steady diet, especially with commercials mixed-in, makes for passive kids who are seeking entertainment, rather than creating it.

Popular magazines focus on what Hollywood stars are doing, how they act, and where they live. Articles in these magazines primarily talk about three things: how to dress and look better than ever, how to talk and get a certain boyfriend or girlfriend, and superficial advice for very personal concerns or problems. A recent teen magazine had these three cover stories: "Kissing the Good, the Bad, and the Ugly," "How to Get Close Without Going All the Way," and "Get Them All Calling You."

There are teenagers who do not pay attention to these magazines, but through friends the majority seem to know what's being talked about in them. Their glitz, glamour, and the general tone of the articles make them inviting and easy to read. They give quick advice, and even quicker styles. Their fast-paced, superficial style keeps kids focused on what's new, rather than what's best.[2]

---

2   R. Pirsig

Callie (13)

"Mom, I'm not a pervert." Callie's words echoed in my waiting room when I entered to introduce myself. Her head dropped and her mother looked away as I invited them into my office. Their discomfort eased only slightly as Callie began talking about her school and her Wednesday night youth group.

Her eyes sparkled when she described her friends and the tricks they played on each other. Her demeanor quickly changed when her mother explained why Callie's probation officer required therapy. Callie had been babysitting three neighborhood children when things got carried away.

"I don't know why you even played such a stupid game with those kids," her mother abruptly stated.

"I didn't mean to, Mom," Callie said softly.

"Well," her mother continued, "you certainly weren't taking very good care of them."

"Mom, I know," Callie responded.

After I asked Mom to listen, Callie gathered her strength and told me what had happened.

"I was just doing what they wanted to do because we were bored, but now I know I should've stopped it sooner." She looked down as she spoke.

"We were playing a game called 'Truth or Dare' and asking each other to do dumb things, like stand on your head and try to drink water, and eat some dirt out of a potted plant. And then Johnny, who's 4, started dancing around and shaking his hips. His sisters—Sarah, who's 6, and Amy, who's 7—were laughing so hard that they fell back on the floor. I thought it was funny, too, and I didn't think anything of it when Amy dared him to do it on me. I lay back on the floor with Amy and Sarah, and Johnny danced and stepped across our stomachs. Then Sarah dared me to hump on Johnny. He laughed at first, but then said he couldn't breathe, so I got off. Then Johnny dared me to show my boobies, and I just pulled my shirt down a little bit. Amy dared Sarah to act like a baby and suck my nipple, so I let her. They all laughed and kind of jumped on top of me. We all just pretended we were humping, and then I dared Johnny to pee in the plants. He made a mess, so the girls screamed and went outside to play. I put a video on for Johnny and cleaned the mess up."

Callie was silent for a moment. Her mother was shaking her head while looking out the window.

"After I cleaned up, I felt weird inside, and when I sat next to Johnny to watch his video, he moved away from me and said, 'Don't squish me again.' I felt so bad I could hardly look at their mom when she came home."

"Callie, what were you thinking?" her mom shouted.

Callie looked back at her mother, with tears in her eyes. "Mom..."

Eventually, Callie's mother learned to listen to her daughter without constantly being angry and making judgmental statements. She finally heard her daughter when she said, "Mom, you always get angry and don't want to talk, or else you just walk away from me." The listening brought to light a life she did not realize her daughter experienced. Her friends were always trying to find new ways to show their cleavage, having contests to see who could move the most provocatively at school dances. On one occasion, at a friend's party, a boy grabbed and twisted her breasts just to get her friends to laugh.

Callie lived in a world that her mother didn't see, and only with respectful listening did she finally understand. After a significant amount of time, dealing with Callie's own victimizations and sexual confusions, she came full circle to apologize and resolve her own inappropriate behavior. She would not have had the chance to do that if her mother hadn't learned to listen, to heal her own victim feelings, and to learn a different meaning of sexuality.

Another area of influence on our children and teenagers is music. Some of the rock groups they listen to and the music videos they watch have a decidedly sexist tone. In these types of videos, women are presented as either helpless or provocatively flaunting their bodies. Men are presented as chasers and aggressive tough guys. Each of their showy roles are acted out within a myriad of quick flashing scenes of unusual or sexualized dance moves. All of this flaunting and toughness is combined with the beat of the song to present a mini-sexualized show of their melody.

These music videos strike quickly and hit deeply. An emotional, sexualized response is usually sparked, and without limited viewing and appropriate talks to keep it in perspective, the stimulated energy is merely put on hold or stored away. This contained, sexualized energy can easily be tapped into and released when teenagers are with peers, or it unconsciously expresses itself to form and maintain very sexist and narrow beliefs about women and men.

The expression of teenager sexual energy and curiosities is inescapable, not only because it is an important part of their personal development, but also because it is being constantly stoked and prodded by an over-sexualized media. This media includes advertising, music videos, and television programs, all easily accessible, and usually all with unlimited viewing. That is part of the grooming process: setting-up teenagers with sparks of sexualized energy without clear communication or age-appropriate outlets. Sexualized messages surround all of us, and if we, as parents, are not telling our kids the complete truth about sex, they become lost in the swirling and ever-present negative sexualizations in our society.

Subtle Influences

A subtle influence that unintentionally leads our children and teenagers into negative sexual exposure is overly strict or scared parents. In their attempts to protect their children, they unknowingly block complete learning by silently controlling too much of their kids' world. They believe that if their kids learn too much about sex they will engage in sexual intimacy. Studies conducted on kids who have had complete sex education courses do not bear out this assumed connection. There have been several surveys, most notably by D. Kirby in 1994, correlating accurate sex education with more sexual activity among teenagers.[3] Although he found some traditional sex education programs and those taught by certain teachers to have no positive or negative effect on teenagers' sexual behavior, he discovered that the programs most effective at delaying sexual involvement combined complete sex education with lessons in how to resist social and peer pressure. Open dialogue, complete communication, and practice role playing with peers has a very positive effect on how teenagers deal with sexuality. In my practice, teenagers who have accurate knowledge and open dialogue with their parents appear calmly confident regarding sexuality and

---

3   Kirby, D.

their decisions. Kids who do not experience open dialogue with their parents or have not had comprehensive sex education appear nervous and vulnerable when sexuality is discussed. These different reactions are noticed among peers and used to begin friendships, ignore someone, or take advantage or make fun of those less confident.

It is important for parents to not let their fears and attempts at protecting them get in the way of healthy and respectful sexuality education because most kids are still exposed to the sexually provocative media. It is natural curiosity to seek out and explore something that is being kept from them. The problem, when their parents aren't talking, is that their eventual learning about sex is in secret or through the media, and therefore learned at a negative and narrow-minded level. If their friends are talking or joking about sex, they will listen. If a particular movie depicts sexual scenes, they will watch it. If someone has magazines with sexual pictures, they will look at them. In effect, they are learning about sexuality in piecemeal fashion and their struggle to understand it remains an incomplete and on-going challenge.

Not talking frequently to children and teenagers about healthy sexuality is giving too much licensure to those in the media who are talking about it. They deal with it indirectly and are disrespectfully provocative, but at least they're dealing with it. They are not afraid of the subject, which, of course, is more than what many teenagers can say about their parents. The media knows that if kids are watching, regardless of their various negative sexual messages, their products will, and do, sell. Non-talking parents give an incredible amount of power to the media, and indirectly keep their kids focused on influences outside of their family.

A seemingly fun and innocuous activity that really is another subtle form of sexist grooming is cheerleaders and athletes. When the cheerleading squad has only girls as its members and the school team has only boys as its players, their participation only reinforces sexist roles. The same is true for dance lines that include only one sex, teams that prohibit the opposite sex, and any activity that has as its sole purpose one-sex showiness. Whenever girls band together to display or show off feminine traits or boys come together to show off masculine traits, the underlying message is powerful; girls are primarily meant to display their looks, and boys are primarily meant to show off their strength or accomplishments. One solution to this rigid and out-dated sexist role playing is to have co-ed cheerleading squads with equal presence at boys and girls team events. Anything short of co-ed opportunities is merely subtle grooming in the sexualization of our young people.

Recently, some states have had a growing number of schools drop their cheerleading programs. They've stated reasons such as these: it's a headache to run, it's not really a sport, and the participants aren't really doing athletics. These reasons are shallow and miss the point. Cheerleading can be fun, athletic, and respectful in those schools that encourage and maintain equal participation for girls and boys. Equality of girls' and boys' representation in school activities is the main, respectful alternative to one-sided, sexist roles.

In essence, the trick and the influence of the media is fortified by parents and families who don't regularly talk about sexuality. This is usually not intentional, because it has crept up slowly over the years as parents have gotten busier trying to provide for their families. With two parents working to accomplish this feat, children and teenagers have had more unsupervised time to watch television, movies, advertising, and videos. Some of these forms of entertainment and exposure to the media can, and should be limited, but the real solution is in counterbalancing what they take in through open conversations, healthy family experiences, and exposure to respectful, age-appropriate and caring sexuality.

Sexual Provocativeness

Alluring sexual provocativeness is no longer just for fun or joking around. It is deep in our minds, and it doesn't belong there in such a disrespectful manner. We have become unconsciously accustomed to the subtle and blatant sexualizations of the media that their indirect and negative provocativeness has become the norm. Because sexuality is such an important aspect of our lives, it is always just below the surface, waiting for expression and acknowledgement. Without frequently dealing with our sexuality in open and healthy ways, our natural drive for expression has nowhere to turn except our media's superficially created norms.

Recently some friends brought us to a professional basketball game. During halftime, the teams' cheerleading dancers pulled several kids from the audience to join in. Out of seven kids, the one boy who got the most attention and audience applause was the one who moved his hips. He was gyrating in all directions and the crowd cheered louder as the dancers highlighted him. Everyone seemed to be laughing and having fun. I sat back and looked around at the kids in my section. A few were laughing and some were talking and pointing, but most of the children I saw were sitting perfectly still; mesmerized by what they were watching. I wasn't sure if they were in shock or just curious, but their faces looked sullen. It seemed like they weren't enjoying what was going on. The adults in my section were hysterical with laughter, except for a few such as myself. We had reservations about what we saw: adults laughing and obviously enjoying something sexually provocative, and many kids watching in stillness. They appeared to be lost by what they were watching, and they reacted quietly, most likely because it was uncomfortable for them.

The kind of behavior we saw at that basketball game is no longer playing; it's for real—adult female dancers showing off sexually provocative poses and an audience encouraging children to do the same. Most of the people in that arena seemed to have been groomed and trained to enjoy and laugh at sexually provocative behavior. When a whole arena is behind that kind of provocativeness, even in front of their children, it has been too deeply ingrained in our society. It has become a part of our lives, our entertainment, and unfortunately, our family activities. It was not good judgment in the arena that day, and it's exactly that kind of non-thinking that subtly grooms our children to accept and enjoy sexually provocative behavior. I did not see acceptance and enjoyment on many of the younger kids' faces that day. It was stillness, curiosity, and reservation. They were being introduced to the grooming process, and therefore they were naturally hesitant.

Understanding Our Kids' Developmental Process

It is important to remember what the prominent developmental psychologists, Jean Piaget and Erik H. Erickson, discovered in their work with children. In Piaget's research, he found that young children—ages three to six—emulate what they see without the cognitive ability to understand the idea or meaning behind it.[4] 4 Therefore, visual pictures

---

4   J. Piaget, Six Psychological Studies, p.20

and experiences are more powerful than words. Parents can talk as much as they want to about how a certain model in an advertisement doesn't act so provocatively in real life, but internally, their children will remember the visual image, not their parent's words. A child at a young age can repeat their parents' words, but true learning occurs primarily through visual images and personal experiences. Without a parent showing appropriate affection toward others in caring ways their child has no internal image or experience to refute the provocative images of the model.

Erik H. Erickson also found that young children, before the age of seven, "cannot hold on or let go with discretion," and, "the child is at no time more ready to learn quickly and avidly than during this period of development."[5] Young children anxiously take in what they see and hear, and they do not yet have the ability to completely discriminate fact from fiction or prioritize necessary and unnecessary information. One particular boy I worked with was waking in fear every night, thinking that dinosaurs were trying to eat him. He would run into his parents' bed, crying and telling them to lock all the doors. His parents repeatedly told their son, "Ryan, dinosaurs aren't alive anymore, so you don't have to worry." But Ryan looked incredulously at his parents and replied, "Yeah, I know, but they're on the other side of the world." The only approach that helped Ryan slowly begin to sleep through the night was assurances that his parents would always protect him, and telling him stories of friendly dinosaurs that were bigger than the hungry dinosaurs. It wasn't until the end of Ryan's first year in school that he was able to smile at his earlier fears. If we do not relate to our children on their level by giving them healthy images and respectful experiences regarding their bodies, they will remain extremely vulnerable to our society's provocative images.

Both Piaget and Erickson state that children, ages eight to eleven, are in a calmer developmental stage. Their main focus is to please adults and gain acceptance for adhering to the rules or norms. It is a time when parents need to lightly comment on sexuality issues and answer sex education questions easily and comfortably. If a child perceives any discomfort or tension surrounding sexuality, they are more likely to not ask or talk about the topic for the sake of being a good girl or boy.

---

5   E. Erickson, *Childhood & Society*, p. 252-258

The ongoing basis for open communication and comfortable dialogue is either nurtured and expanded during this stage or it is neglected and lost.

Piaget's research found that children develop a more formal or broader way of thinking when they are in early adolescence. They see the world and begin to understand that they have the ability to fit themselves into it. In his research, Erickson states that often a young adolescent's desire to fit in is so strong that "to keep themselves together, they temporarily over-identify to the point of apparent complete loss of [their own] identity, with the heroes of cliques and crowds."[6] In other words, a young teenager's desire and need for acceptance and belonging with their peers is so powerful that they can temporarily abandon their own ideals and values. If kids are watching television and reading current magazines they will talk about it with their peers and often blindly imitate behaviors of their friendship group. The important point when parenting kids at this stage is to allow some experimentation and peer playfulness, but hold firmly to family time, one-on-one talks before they go to bed, and appropriate affection. As parents, we need to remember that it is not our judgmental statements or disapproving expressions that move our kids through a particular developmental state. It is our enduring love for them as an individual, support for what they want to try, attentiveness to their needs, holding them accountable for negative behaviors, and a sincere interest and involvement in their lives and activities.

Slanted Focus

The sexualized focus in our society is abusive to women and men. It discounts women as individuals by continually giving the message that the most important attribute is to look pretty and be sexually attractive. It discounts men as individuals by giving the impression that they always strive for and need sexual gratification. It also discounts our children's and teenagers' learning and mature development by presenting a skewed picture of personal relationships. This is accomplished whenever the media use men and women and highlight their personal sexuality in only provocative or alluring ways. The sexual intimacy and emotional closeness that happens naturally between two people who care about

---

6   E. Erickson, Childhood & Society, p. 262

each other is used out of context. Instead of showing couples looking at each other in caring ways, they display men and women in very sexually provocative and intense poses. These models or actors are doing it to sell a product or get higher television ratings, not to express caring sexual feelings with a loved one. When the personal, intimate aspect of a relationship is taken out of a loving context and publicly displayed in an exaggerated way, it misleads our young people. They don't learn that caring, sexual expression is for private moments between themselves and their loved one, rather it shows them how to use something personal and sexual to get what they want. Whether it's to sell a product, to get people to buy a magazine, or to belong to a particular health club, the message is skewed: look sexy and get what you want.

The harm is done to our children and teenagers when they witness these types of superficial displays day after day. Children are mesmerized by them and therefore can't pull away, and it pulls so strongly at a teenager's increasing sexual curiosities that they don't want to turn away. Our kids' primary developmental task is to learn, so they listen, watch, and imitate. What kids take in, they will unconsciously integrate and repeat. This scenario is damaging to our children's natural learning processes and fosters confusion and immaturity. The presentation and attitude of the media, which promotes sex as a thing to play with, tease with, or use it anyway you want to, is one of the most destructive and pervasive obstacles to the healthy and normal emotional development of American kids today.

The only place where the media cannot have such dangerously subtle effects is where the child's or teenager's personal experiences are very different from what is displayed in the media. Kids who have actually experienced respectful, open dialogue on sexuality and the casual changing of clothes within their own families are the individuals who very likely will not be negatively affected by media hype. They may have their attention caught when the advertisements are shown, but their real-life experiences have given them something different. This experiential difference is the significant growing piece that provides emotional safety and affords them the chance at real maturity. The media is encountered, but it can't hold the core of their personalities because a child's personality can be formed deeper and stronger through actual life experiences. Each age level for our kids has its own age appropriate situations to be experienced. For example, toddlers and young children can comfortably change clothes or use the bathroom with the door open in their home. This experientially teaches them bodily respect and non-sexualized nudity prior to learning about procreation. Middle-aged children can comfortably understand and talk about body parts and how they work normally and during intimacy. This gives them a visual picture and knowledge beyond what the media is teasing about; therefore, these kids have the ability to avoid the media's tricks. Teenagers are more comfortable with respectful sexuality books in the home and only talking occasionally about sexuality. If a parent is available to talk and periodically makes comments or asks questions, their parent and teenage communication lines will remain intact. Most ages are comfortable with respectful sexuality books around the house and parents who communicate in non-pushy or non-pressuring ways. The media will continue to bombard the different age levels to get their attention, for their attitudes, and create mindsets, and the only effective countering of these types of media games are actual life experiences that are completely different, open, and caring. If we can make these differences for our kids, their maturity will develop in easily recognizable ways. If we let the media give our kids their first, and on-going exposure to the numerous aspects of sexuality, we will see our children and teenagers falter in their emotional development and become confused in their learning.

B.) The Outcome

The effects of current sexual presentations on our children and teenagers

Everyday we encounter television, radio, newspapers, magazine covers, and billboards. As adults, we are unconsciously and negatively affected by the sexually provocative nature of these presentations in the same way our children are affected; however, they are more vulnerable. We see an advertisement with supermodels, and usually shake our heads and let it go. Our kids see supermodels and athletes and say to themselves, "I'm going to be just like them." Their reactions are different than adults because they are young, impressionable, and dreaming about their futures. Unlike adults, they don't ignore most of what they see in the media; they strive for it.

Kids who obtain most of their information on sexuality from the media are vulnerable to the shallowness and swaying of trends. As Ansuini and Woite pointed out in their 1996 study reported in *Adolescence*, kids with confusion and superficial sexuality information as their basis are noticeably delayed in their personal maturity when compared to kids who have experienced open and complete sexuality information.[7] A lack of complete sexual knowledge keeps our children and teenagers guessing and taking in as much of the media as they can. It is this type of superficial and empty media information that holds our kids down and stagnant in their attempts to learn. Although the issue is complex, there are specific and significant negative effects our sexually saturated media has on ourselves, our children, and our teenagers.

The unperfect body syndrome

We have all seen the commercials and billboards of male and female models. At first we looked in awe. Then we got used to them and hardly noticed them. Now, we turn and passively accept what advertisers do to us. The same thought runs through our heads and we hardly remember thinking it: "The models look great; I never will."

---

7   Ansuini

We may occasionally make side comments about these presentations, but the biggest mistake we make is not talking about the opposite side of these bodily displays with our children and teenagers. We may joke about it and try to laugh it off, but we don't counterbalance that kind of display advertising. We don't talk about what a small part that kind of surface focus actually plays in a caring relationship, and we don't comment on or compliment respectful affection between people in our lives or the occasionally appropriate movie. We are mostly silent, and the pattern of our children and teenagers seeking and working for the perfect body or looking cool goes on. Many parents' attitude is "We lived through it and they probably will too."

However, the steady dose of well-shaped bodies and perfectly-dressed models continually and subconsciously reminds us and our kids that we are not one of the beautiful people. With so much attention on surface-focused media, people, and entertainment, this shallow, yet powerful message rarely gets challenged. As Kim Chernin in her 1981 book, *The Obsession: Reflections on the Tyranny of Slenderness* states, "The obsession with losing weight, regulating diet, monitoring the body, measuring it, weighing it, scrutinizing it, punishing it, rewarding it on occasion for having succeeded in reducing itself was not yet considered an obsession."[8] Girls and women are not always aware that what they're doing to be accepted may in fact be emotionally harmful. Our society has placed so much emphasis on the "perfect body syndrome" that it becomes increasingly difficult for girls and women to pull away because it has become the only way too many men accept them. Over prolonged periods of time, this syndrome affects our children and teenagers and unconsciously hinders their independent thinking. It also blocks their desire to stand up and speak out when they feel uncomfortable or different from what is portrayed as "perfect" because they don't see adults taking a stand and showing them that there is a different way.

Generally, this type of display advertising doesn't affect us significantly if it is received in small doses. However, continual exposure over many years is destructive. We can see this in our society's obsession with fashion and money spent on new clothes to enhance an accepted look. We can see the dysfunctional extreme in our teenage girls who become anorexic or bulimic. We see it on our teenage boys who are

8   Kim Chernin

spending a lot of money on tennis shoes, cologne, and haircuts. Some of these things are innocuous, but when done repeatedly or without other real life experiences, children and teenagers tend to lose sight of what really counts for the sake of surface looks and cool behavior.

Molly (15)

"All I can say is, if I had a bod like Sheila I'd be getting asked to our school dances. She's a bimbo, but guys don't care. They go for the bitchin' bods."

These were Molly's first words in response to her mom's order, "Tell him why we're here." Molly's mom had made the appointment because she was worried about Molly's recent obsession with dieting and working out. Molly and a group of her friends were "exercising and comparing their bodies and weights far too often to be normal," her mom lamented.

Molly snapped back, "I don't care what you say, Mom. You don't know what it's like and I'm sure you did the same thing when you were my age."

"I did not. I've always accepted the fact that I'm bigger-boned, and you'll have to accept it, too."

"Well, I'm not, and don't tell me I'm bigger boned. I can still look good."

"Of course you can, honey. I'm just saying don't over do it, and if guys don't like you the way you are, then they're not really good guys."

"Mom...don't give me your lecture on guys."

Their conversation went on until I asked Molly to talk about how hard it was at her school, especially with the boys. She began slowly, but the more she could see her mom was listening, the more she revealed. She talked about when her long-time friend Scott began flirting with a girl on the cheerleading squad, and how even though their lockers were close, as the year went on he hardly acknowledged her anymore. She talked about thinking nothing of it except that it was normal friendship changes until she overheard two of her girlfriends. They had been asked to a recent school dance and Molly hadn't. Their comment in the school lounge had something to do with "me getting on an exercise program."

With tears, Molly told her mom how just last week some guys were teasing her and her friends about hosting a "wet-butt" contest rather than a "wet T-shirt" contest. "And it wasn't a compliment, Mom!"

"But Molly, you're not overweight," her mom said.

"Well, obviously the guys think I am…"

"Oh no, Molly, that's not…"

"Mom, give it a rest," Molly interrupted. "I don't have a choice."

At the end of the session Molly made it clear that she did not want to schedule another appointment and saw no need for counseling. She seemed to feel a little better knowing that her mother had listened, but only reluctantly accepted my recommendations for a dietician to at least monitor her new eating and exercising plan.

Even though Molly felt like it, she was not alone. Everyday in America, teenage girls are subtly or directly put down or discounted for their body type and looks. They try hard to compensate for what guys or the media says they don't have, or have too much of. It is really a personal attack on their identities, and it hurts them and affects their self-esteem more than we know. Listening to Molly tell her mother how hard it was for her in school helped me realize that although this was one girl's story, it is the plight of many.

2.) Maintaining discomfort with sexual talk.

Current media presentations keep us feeling uncomfortable when sex is the topic. Naturally, when sex is not talked about openly we would be somewhat uncomfortable dealing with the subject. However, instead of attempting to talk about sexuality in respectful ways, adults have become silent. Our society as a whole has acquiesced to the media on the subject of sexuality. Not only has the media enjoyed being the only ones dealing with sexuality, they have taken it one step further: Playing with our existing avoidance and having a field day with it.

They have interjected more discomfort into the topic of sex with words like, "nasty," "dirty," and even "it hurts so good." Songs play off of this discomfort by mixing words. One music video says that although it's nasty, she could learn to like it. The attitude that prevails, due to these words and phrases, simply reinforces the barriers surrounding sexual topics. People will even laugh at someone who attempts a sincere discussion on sexual matters—not because it's funny, but because they themselves are so uncomfortable with the topic. It has been ingrained in them that to discuss sex is "nasty," "dirty," or "weird." These well-groomed attitudes are powerful blockers to an extremely important and personal aspect of our lives.

Teenagers have a similar reaction as the media to their parents' avoidance. Because sex is not talked about frequently in caring, respectful ways by the adults in their lives, they go along with the prevailing media mood. They laugh about it—tease each other with it. They have fun with it because at least they're dealing with a topic that needs expression—disrespectfully, maybe, and just on the surface, but more frequently than the close-mouthed adults in their lives are dealing with it.

Teenagers who need to feel some sense of know-how and new identity naturally hang onto it as something they have that adults don't have. Superficially and one-sided, but at least they're talking.

Frank (15 years old)

Frank attended a therapy appointment with his mom and step-dad of eight years. Both parents made the appointment because, as they stated, "Frank is way too mean to his younger siblings and his sexual comments were gross."

Cindy, Frank's mother, said she was comfortable with the boy's visiting their birth father as long as he kept communicating with her. In the past he would contact the boys out of the blue and they would excitedly tell her about Dad calling and the fun they were going to have, and then often cancel. Now that he agreed to arrange visits through her, not only were the boys on a more even keel in their moods, the visits became more regular. Frank's step-dad agreed and said it seemed that the boys were happier now that they were seeing their father.

Mom and step-dad went on to say that for the past year Frank had become more physical in his teasing and more gross in his remarks about girls and sex.

"He used to just tease them on and off, but now it's constant and he's hitting and pushing them." She went on, "The other day the little ones were watching television and he came in, changed the channel and pushed his brother off the couch so he could sit down."

Step-dad added, "And then his brother started to cry, so Frank called him several names and told him to 'go suck yourself off.' His brother told us later what had happened and Frank basically denied it." While his parents talked of his behavior and their concerns, Frank shook his head and smirked. Then he defended himself by saying, "You guys aren't there to see what actually happened, so you automatically take the younger kid's side."

I had Frank tell me more about his side of things—his interests and what he did with his friends. He was a stocky boy with reddish hair and freckles. His eyes were intense, and when he became angry with his folks he leaned forward in a determined way. When he was finished trying to make a point with his folks, he would look at me and slowly sit back.

He talked of being busy with his friends after school, whether they were throwing a Frisbee around or catching a ride into town to play pool. He admitted to being hard on one of his younger brothers, but only because he was such a baby. Frank believed he had to toughen him up.

As my questions focused more on Frank and his behavior, he also admitted to sometimes making sexual comments. He agreed that at times they were rude or disrespectful, but added "That's just how me and my friends talk." He looked at his step-dad and went on, "I'm sure you did it too, when you were with your friends, and besides, even my dad does it if it's just me and my brother with him. Guys do it and it's no big deal."

Step-dad began to defend himself and Mom started lecturing Frank on having respect for girls. Again, Frank sat back and began shaking his head. In her anger his mom said, "I never taught you to talk that way about girls or women!"

Frank shot back, "You never taught me nothing about girls. I learned it for myself."

Step-dad tried to settle the conversation down. Mom stared at her son, with tears running down her cheeks. Frank sat rigid in his chair, frowning and gazing out the window.

Both Frank and his mother had hurt feelings. Mom, because she was trying hard but couldn't reach her son like she once had. Frank, because he missed his father, and in his hurt and anger he took his feelings out on smaller family members and made inappropriate sexual comments. He had learned them from his father, friends, and the media, and he was vulnerable to making sexual remarks a lifelong habit of expressing his intense emotions. Future therapy sessions would need to include his mom, stepfather, and father, not only to resolve old pain, but also to give Frank and his father a non-victimizing framework for verbalizing sexuality and an interest in girls.

3.) The mistrust factor

Media presentations make our children and teenagers less trustful of their parents because they see them not resolving or dealing with something that makes them uncomfortable. If parents sit uncomfortably silent and feel embarrassed when sex is presented in a movie or television show they are watching with their children; if parents turn away and say "Go ask your mother or father" when kids ask personal sexual questions; if adults tease and joke about their children's and teenagers' attractions for another person; or if adults have trouble looking in a mirror at their own naked bodies, then they have been extremely negatively affected by our media's dealings with sexuality. In avoiding the topic, the same embarrassed silence is passed onto our children; not talking about sexuality in respectful, caring ways is a poor example set by parents. Our young children and teenagers will understandably shy away from sexual conversations or questions. Without adults talking somewhat comfortably about sexuality or inviting questions there are no openings for our young ones. In effect, they are doomed to the same silencing power of discomfort that the adults in their lives have been living under.

This puzzling combination of seeing their parents feel uncomfortable and not talking about it confuses younger children. They end up holding in experiences because their parents are lost. In this case, almost all children will deny, forget, or avoid the experience in order to preserve at least the illusion that their parents can handle anything. Whenever the subject of sex arises, these parents uncomfortably just try to get past it and their young children just try to forget it.

However, young teenagers cannot let go of experiences that are uncomfortable for their parents as easily. They are developing mentally and emotionally on personal issues and such experiences are logged into who can be trusted and who can't. Most teenagers will automatically log sexuality as a topic not to be discussed with parents, but many will be angry because it's another area where they can't count on their parents while they're growing up. Because they don't trust their parents with the topic, they go elsewhere. Parents who are accustomed to ignoring the sexuality topic have also lost their ability to see their teenagers' natural curiosity and inquisitive minds concerning other personal issues. Therefore, feeling close or connected with their parents is a distant memory for many teenagers.

Time magazine, in their June 15, 1998 issue, stated that in 1986, 8% of teenagers learned about sex from their parents.[9] In 1998, 7% of teenagers surveyed said they learned about sex from their parents. It also said 45% learned about sex from their friends, and 29% learned sex from television. Parents of teenagers in America aren't even close to television or peers when it comes to teaching and guiding their children and teenagers on sex education and sexuality issues.

This is just the tip of the iceberg for kids in America. When parents don't take the time, effort and responsibility to address the personal topic of sex, it not only leaves kids at the mercy of the media and incompletely-informed peers, but it can and does erode their trust and respect for relying on their parents for other important personal topics. Talking about sex within families has a very profound and positive effect on kids, and therefore not addressing it leaves gaping holes and misunderstandings in their knowledge base and maturity level.

Another comment that the *Time* article stated was that of the teenagers surveyed, "Most kids lament the fact that their parents either don't talk about sex at all, or make it boring and filled with warnings." The key is to not lecture kids, but rather to talk with them, make it fun, and admit that you don't know everything. Looking up sexual terms together or exploring each family member's opinion on an issue without trying to make everything one answer is invaluable for kids.

Parents are the architects of family communication, and in their avoidance of the sexuality topic they have unknowingly neglected to build the necessary bridges to conversation. As a result, young children keep trying to put it out of their minds. Teenagers struggle with the ignored discomfort and go elsewhere for expression and learning. Sadly,

---

9   Time Magazine, 1998

these children and teenagers have learned from their parents' avoidance and maintained discomforts. Mistrust has entered into the parent/child relationship and an opportunity for a continued and lasting closeness has been lost.

Amy (16) and Anna (14)

Barbara called, asking for an appointment because her daughters were in danger of becoming sexual in their boyfriend relationships. With some questioning, she clarified that on several occasions she had overheard her 14-year-old and 16-year-old daughters talking about "doing their boyfriends." She said that she got nowhere with the girls when telling them that sex is only for procreation.

At the first appointment it was difficult for Amy (16) and Anna (14) to not laugh when their mother talked. They also struggled to even look at me when I asked them questions. After a few minutes, Barbara gave up, looked at me, and in tears said, "See what I mean? They don't even want to understand." At this, both girls became quiet and lowered their heads.

I asked questions about whether or not they had introduced their boyfriends to their mother; if they, as a family, ever had family meetings about sex issues; and if they were familiar with birth control. They answered "No" to each question, except Amy said that birth control was "the pill." The girls said they had had sex education classes in school years ago, but the teacher was embarrassed and didn't care if they just talked quietly to each other.

With Barbara listening to the questions I asked, the girls slowly gave me a picture of their lives. Amy said she used to talk with her mom, but when she began junior high her mother only gave lectures: the same three lectures about staying away from drugs, don't skip classes, and save yourself for marriage. She enjoyed volleyball and going out with her girlfriends, but she was afraid to admit that she had a boyfriend.

Anna said she loved junior high school, switching classes, and seeing all her friends between classes. She loved art, but she didn't always show her mom because some of it embarrassed her. She said her mom would frown and not want to talk about what the artwork meant. She liked a boy, but she wasn't sure he liked her yet. She always talked to her older sister, so she never had any real questions for her mom.

Turning some of my questions to Barbara, she wiped her tears and said she was very scared for her girls. She had always wanted them to be safe, and after their father died she felt totally alone. The girls were 8 and 10 when his third heart attack took him.

"When he died, I made a promise to never let anything bad happen to our babies, but I never knew it would be so hard. Since they've become teenagers, they don't even listen to my warnings."

I asked Barbara if she would be comfortable using the phrase "sharing information," rather than "giving warnings." She stopped and looked at me. "What do you mean?" I explained the difference between assuming the worst and continually giving warnings, and believing that teenagers and parents can share information or understandings in order to come up with good personal decisions.

Barbara asked how they could do that. I suggested three family meetings at my office. The purpose would be for her to learn about her daughters' daily lives, to know their opinion, and for Amy and Anna to know what their mother had learned from the ups and downs of her own life.

The appointments went slowly, because the girls were hesitant to talk and Barbara was so afraid for her daughters' safety that she found it hard to listen. I recommended that they attend another three sessions in order to come to more understanding and compromises. Over time, Barbara was able to listen and accept her daughters' opinions and values because she had the courage to resolve her own fears.

During several individual talks, Barbara spoke of her own uncomfortable experiences with an overbearing, drinking father. "One time, when I was about 8 or 9, I remember hiding in the closet with my mother because we heard him yelling in the garage. We knew he was coming into the house, so we hid to avoid his temper. It rarely got physical, but he did grab my arm hard sometimes and lead me to my bedroom. After he slammed the door and went to the kitchen to shout at my mom, I still didn't know why I was being punished."

She took my suggestion and wrote in a daily, private journal. Many memories flooded back to her, and through tears she told me, "I was so embarrassed—and I guess afraid of my dad—that I never had my friends come to my house. I would do things, but always at their homes."

Barbara hesitantly joined a women's support group, but within three meetings was speaking comfortably about it, and later, she occasionally joined some of the women after group for coffee. Her personal work also had positive effects in communication with her daughters. Instead of talking about different personal topics with dogmatic statements, she was beginning to listen first and then calmly state her beliefs. Because she was doing the work of facing and expressing her own difficult experiences, she was better able to balance her emotions while talking with her daughters. Prior to resolving her past personal issues, Barbara, like many parents who have not faced their own past experiences in a direct and healing way, was severely hindered in her attempts to have real dialogue with children or teenagers. Emotionally unhealed or unresolved parents have a tendency to be too close and overbearing toward their children, or too emotionally unavailable or distant. Neither is helpful or healthy for parents who are trying to raise mature kids.

The girls became more open and comfortable sharing with their mother once they saw that she wouldn't judge them or just give warnings. To be listened to helped the girls immensely. They both eventually came out of their protective shells and engaged in real dialogue with their mother. At the end of their 14th appointment Anna commented, "I don't think we need to come here anymore because we have family meetings at home now, and the other day we even had one about sex topics." Amy and Barbara both laughed, and this time it wasn't from being nervous.

If Barbara had not embraced her own issues in a personally direct way, she would have remained rigid in her opinions and true dialogue with her daughters would never have occurred. However, in her desire to become close again with her daughters, she had the courage to turn inward and change. Without Barbara doing her own work, the distance between her and her daughters would have only widened, and discussing personal topics like sexuality would have remained out of reach.

4.) Glitz or good?

Media presentations can take our children and teenagers away, mentally, if parents allow unlimited television, electronic games, and videos. The more exciting and fast-paced advertisers make their commercials and presentations, the more our children and teenagers watch them and then expect that kind of action in their own lives. Sitting around the house and talking or playing a board game just doesn't compare to what they've seen on television. As a result, they are drawn to look outside their own families. Typically, children can do things comfortably with family members. Teenagers, on the other hand, look for life outside their families and are usually uncomfortable doing family activities. Certainly, teenagers ought to be given the independence to do a lot with their friends, but parents should never let family activities that include their teenagers fall off their list.

Many families I see in therapy have as one of the biggest concerns of parents who allow unlimited viewing of television and electronic games is that their children or teenagers are either spacey and unmotivated, or too hyper and fidgety. Children and teenagers react differently to media overload, but often it is to the extreme, and parents are rightfully worried. The glitz and chaotic action they view daily makes the media much more interesting than the reality of their own lives. However, growth and maturity can occur only in their family relationships, individual endeavors, and their interactions with people of all ages outside of their own families. It does not happen in front of glitzy, fast-moving media presentations. I believe that every day that a child spends more than one hour watching television, their parent will have to spend two hours trying to undo the damage, re-connect again, or argue about values.

Tom (15 years old)

Tom was court ordered to my therapy program for kissing and touching the breasts of a young girl. Amy was 12; Tom was 15. He told me that the incident happened at a friend's house after school one day. His friend, Ben, had told him earlier in the day that he knew a girl who thought he was cute. He was going home after school with his girlfriend and wondered if Tom would come over too. If he could, Ben would tell his girlfriend to ask Amy to come over also.

Tom said he was nervous and didn't get back to Ben until after lunch. Ben said it would be fun, and no big deal, so Tom agreed. When Tom got to Ben's house, Ben, his girlfriend, and Amy were all laughing and talking in the living room.

"I could tell she liked me because she got embarrassed as soon as I walked in. When I said hi, I got even more nervous because she was very pretty. I realized I liked her too, but I didn't know if she could tell."

"Ben got us all some pop and then he left with his girlfriend. I wasn't sure where he went, but probably to his bedroom."

Tom continued in a quieter tone. "We ran out of things to say in a couple of minutes. She kept smiling in an embarrassed way and I still didn't know what to talk about, so I said 'Here, take my hand.'"

Tom went on to say that he led Amy into another bedroom and sat on the bed. He said he still felt awkward and at a loss for words, so he just started kissing her.

"It seemed like the thing to do. She wasn't talking and I wasn't either, and my friend was alone with his girlfriend in another room, probably making out."

Tom began to look more confused or puzzled as he spoke.

"I don't know why, but then I slowly laid back on the bed with her and automatically started going up her shirt. It felt weird—like I was in a dream-world or something—but I didn't know what else to do."

His face turned more sullen as he related what happened next.

"Suddenly, I could tell she was upset because she kind of stopped kissing back. She was real still and I could tell something wasn't right."

Tom finished his story by saying, "So I sat-up and said 'Let's go back and get our pop.' She came right behind me and we just watched television until Ben and his girlfriend came downstairs.

They saw me and Amy sitting there and Ben pointed his thumb up in the air and said, 'Hey, how did it go, man?'

I just said, 'Good, real good.' And he nodded and said 'Hey, hey, way to go.'

I asked several questions and found out that shortly after Ben and his girlfriend returned to the living room, Tom left. He also said he felt kind of weird and bad about it because he liked Amy and didn't know if things would work out. He didn't know if he would feel comfortable seeing her again and didn't even know her phone number.

About two weeks later, Tom said the police came to his home, interviewed him, and charged him with 4th degree sexual misconduct. Apparently, Amy liked him too, but when she hadn't heard from him, she felt used and told a friend about what happened. That friend told a school counselor, who in turn talked to Amy, and subsequently reported the incident to the authorities.

Tom said the whole police and court thing scared him and he wasn't sure why Amy didn't call him if she liked him so much. He said it seemed like they both kind of did it together, so why was he being charged? He said it was hardest on his parents because he couldn't talk about such things with them anyway. His dad was so mad it was best not to say anything until he cooled down, and Mom just cried and made him feel like a pervert.

Toward the end of our session, Tom kept shaking his head and saying, "I just wish I could've gotten to know her in the regular way before any of this happened."

It appeared to me that Tom's heart may have been in the right place, but he was immature for his age. He allowed himself to get in over his head, and he lacked the communication that practiced openness at home can bring about. To even be with a girl three years his junior in such a way gave away his immaturity and need for decision-making skills and age-appropriate peer interaction. The behavior, which was very disrespectful and victimizing, was formed within the glitz of Tom's life. Be cool on the surface, do what everybody else is doing for fun, and everything will be all right. His immaturity, combined with his artificial glitzy education, was Tom's and his victim's worst experience. Glitz is not good; it's a set-up, and often times that's dangerous.

Children and teenagers read their parents very well. They know when to ask for something so they will most likely get it. They know when their parents are rambling because they really don't know the answer. And above all, they know when not to talk because their parents are nervous or uncomfortable with the topic. The majority of children and teenagers see their parents react this way when sexual topics arise. Their parents may nervously laugh. They may say "Go ask your mother"—or father—or they may even get more intense, as if something is wrong.

Children and teenagers may not know what's going on in their parents' minds, but they do know what their parents are feeling: scared, uncomfortable, nervous, and maybe even confused. Our offspring are wise enough to let it go and walk away. Changing the subject or silence also works. But their responses to their parents' fears are clear: keep quiet and don't bring up this topic again.

This pattern hurts parent/child relationships in three ways. One, something important is not being talked about, so the child or teenager does not learn about the many topics of sex. Two, they don't hear and learn the words to talk about sex in a respectful way. And three, children—but especially teenagers—begin to lose respect and trust for their parents. They witness their own parents crumble in front of them, and that's nothing to look up to.

Charlie (15)

Nancy was so worried about her son Charlie's use of sexual slang phrases that she got a referral from his school to make an appointment with me. She would hear him get mad at his younger sister and call her a bitch. On other occasions she would hear him calling his younger brother "gay" when he dropped the baseball or didn't get a hit. She stated that she had repeatedly told him not to use such words, but it didn't seem to help.

She was particularly upset on a recent visit to her sister's home. All of the cousins were in the living room watching a video one evening. She and her sister were visiting and enjoying each other's company in the kitchen. Suddenly, a burst of laughter from the living room interrupted them. Echoing into the kitchen, along with the sounds of laughter, was Charlie's unmistakable voice shouting, "Ah, they're doing the bangin' thing."

It stopped them both momentarily. "My sister and I were dumbfounded. I didn't know what to say or do. There's my sister in as much shock as me, only I was totally embarrassed—not only because of the fact that he even said it, but in front of everyone, including the younger ones."

"Oh, Mom," Charlie spoke up in his defense, "you don't know anything. Everybody says that, or even worse."

"Yes, but you're not everybody and I don't like it when you talk that way."

"Well, I'm not going to change, otherwise my friends will think I'm a geek or something. And besides, I don't talk about it around you, anyway."

Their banter continued above my questions and requests for compromise. The following week Nancy cancelled their appointment and she did not return my call to reschedule. In this case, my intent would have been to assist this mother in not focusing so much on her son's negative speech, but rather giving him a different, broader language to use. I believe this is done when a family engages in a sex education talk together. Such talks are good if they address all aspects of sexuality and use proper, respectful words while still allowing slang word acknowledgement and comparative definition. The more children and teenagers are exposed to and experience sexuality being frequently and respectfully talked about at home, the more chances increase to bridge the gap to their inappropriate expression. And with that bridge, the chance for change is ever more inviting. Other personal issues will likely surface, but to ignore and not broaden her son's artificial cover-ups would lead to never being invited deeper.

Too often teenagers who are sexually uneducated and know or use only slang words or phrases develop an internal callousness to real relationship respect. Their words and attitudes are merely a cover-up for their own lack of knowledge or low self-esteem, and therefore crossing respect boundaries becomes common.

Phillip (16)

Phillip was court-ordered to therapy for verbally sexually harassing his 14-year-old sister, and on two occasions pinching her breast and buttocks. His inappropriate verbal behavior had been happening since he began high school. His pinching behavior began in the last month of the school year. His mother had walked into her daughter's room one evening and saw her crying. She told her mom it was nothing and that she would be all right. However, Phillip's mother persisted, and soon she heard how he would tease her about her body parts and that recently it had turned into pinching. Not only was Phillip's mom shocked, she related that she was confused and saddened by something else her daughter told her. "She said she didn't tell me sooner because that was just the way most guys treated girls. She didn't think her brother would do it to her, but in school when other guys did it, everybody just overlooked it."

Added to this mom's burden of feeling upset and hurt for her own two kids was the new distress and confusion of how kids treat each other. She had much to learn and deal with in the impending family sessions.

Phillip downplayed his behavior in the therapy session. He explained that everybody did it. Friends at school always made comments to girls and sometimes would even poke or pinch their butts. "Even my dad makes comments about women if my mom's not around." He went on to say, "Yeah, well maybe I shouldn't have touched her, but it happened only a couple of times."

Phillip's father was a department foreman by day and a part-time telephone operator two nights a week. He stated that "I don't get much time with my son, so I usually let my wife do the parenting." He was always ready to step in if necessary or if she asked him to, but that didn't happen often. Phillip's mother confirmed his occasional support and added that the kids, including two younger ones, had usually been good. Both Phillip's mom and dad said they were surprised and confused with Phillip's actions and his nonchalant attitude toward his behavior.

As therapy continued, Phillip was visibly not as tense, and with the help of his mother and father in family sessions he verbally began to open up. During group sessions with other boys Phillip talked more and more as the weeks progressed. On one occasion he related that when hanging out with his friends, their talk usually found their ways to comments about his good-looking sister. It wasn't unusual for some of his friends, while Phillip was talking to her, to go behind her and make lewd faces at him. As time went on, he said he just got used to it, and also that "It made me feel cool because of all their attention on me, and because my sister was so attractive." As the group listened, Phillip continued. "Sometimes I forgot myself when I saw her at home when she had her pajamas on or some short shorts, and I would make a comment. Then one time I saw her walking from the bathroom with just a towel wrapped around her and I pinched her butt."

Phillip said it didn't seem like a big deal because, "I thought she screamed in a fun way." At school, he said all the girls were always trying to look good and show off their shape, and "right in my own home, my sister was doing the same thing. And yeah, I guess I got a little carried away, but I only meant it as a compliment." Phillip was not at a point where he could recognize the irony in his words.

After many months of group therapy and sincere dialogue with his sister in family sessions, Phillip slowly began to develop more empathy and a maturity for seeing his sister as a person, rather than just a female object. He was like many boys and young men I treat in therapy. They have learned from the media's norms and presentation of girls, and therefore are caught up in those same negative viewpoints with their peer group and what's cool on the surface. They have no respectful relationship role models to contrast what they see in the media or hear played out in their social life. Phillip was also a boy who missed spending time with his father. Talking about personal topics in sessions, including sexuality and father/son activities, helped both of them to get reconnected and develop more respect for the women in their lives.

The Father/Son Misconnection

There is a subtle and extremely destructive force behind much of the sexually inappropriate behavior perpetrated by boys and young men. It is the absence of or distant relationship these boys and young men have with their fathers. As Lee Beaty, in his 1995 study in the journal *Adolescence* reports, "Father-absent boys have a poorer sense of masculinity, poorer interpersonal relationships, engage in female aggressive behavior, and are more dependent on peers."[10] Over time, these boys who do not experience a closeness with their father compensate where they can, and naturally seek out relationship closeness elsewhere. Unfortunately, these emotionally lost boys and young men too often push for it in their relationships with girls by becoming extremely controlling and overbearing. This brings on disrespectful and abusive behavior on the part of the boys in an attempt to find unmet father needs. His inner loss and emptiness from his own distant father relationship is what unconsciously drives him, and the emotional openness of his girlfriend is where he selfishly places too many of his needs.

In his book *Fatherless America: Confronting our Most Urgent Social Problem*, David Blankenhorn states, "Unless we reverse the trend of fatherlessness, no other set of accomplishments—not economic growth or prison construction or welfare reform or better schools—will succeed

---

10   Lee Beaty

in arresting the decline of child well-being and the spread of male violence."[11] Without emotionally available fathers, as Blankenhorn and numerous other studies have shown, too many sons resort to violence, inappropriate behavior toward females, and are prone to low self-restraint.[12]

Because it is uncomfortable for many fathers to show their gentle side with their son which includes hugs, talking about hurt or scared feelings, and how to compromise in order to be stronger together, these boys lose the important calmness and maturity that a close and connected relationship with their father would provide. A father who frequently lectures or coaches his son is maintaining an emotional distance because he is focusing on minor details or physical performance. If this becomes a habit, a son does not usually feel comfortable or safe to turn to his father during personal difficulties. This occurs because the son has been habitualized to perform well and get things right. With this kind of pressure, it is rare for a son to seek out his father's support when he has made a mistake, is afraid, or needs to cry. The son is so accustomed to his father coaching him how to do something or telling him what he is doing wrong that he buries himself and avoids showing his deeper and more important feelings. Too many boys who are inappropriate toward females have grown up with no experiences of their dad simply listening to them without trying to "fix it." A child's or teenager's learning curve is enhanced and they learn more from their own mistakes if a father frequently provides active listening experiences, rather than "know-it-all lectures." Completely listening to a son's upset feelings and asking what he would like to do about them increases a boy's confidence and maturity more adequately than interrupting and telling him what he should do.

As Michael E. Lamb makes clear in his 1997 work, *The Role of the Father in Child Development*, "The father who is very involved and [exhibits a day-to-day interest in his child's activities] can foster in his child a strong focus of control and sense of responsibility over his or her actions. Through emulating their involved father, children are more likely to demonstrate moral behavior."[13] I believe that any closeness, and therefore moral development, is incomplete if sexuality

11   David Blankenhorn

12   D'Angelo, Bushweller, Biller

13   Michael E. Lamb

talks and the importance of relationship giving and receiving is not an integral part of father and son communication. In therapy, I witness boys struggle and falter in their peer relationships because their father is uninvolved or non-supportive in their lives. These boys desperately need acceptance by their peers, but their internal preoccupation with trying to get right with their own fathers appears to keep them acting immaturely. Although there are multiple factors that contribute to teenage acting-out behaviors, one of the most common is a conflictual or an emotionally distant relationship with a father."[14] Just as a daughter needs a strong connection with her mother through her teenage years in order to identify and develop into a well-adjusted young woman, sons need a strong connection with their fathers to become well-adjusted. Strong mothers help many of these emotionally fatherless boys adjust and do well; however, too many of these boys stagnate and become obtrusive young men. It is incomplete or absent communication that usually maintains an immaturity in these boys, and it is a father's responsibility to create and foster an open relationship with his son in order for true maturation to occur.

Playing, watching, or talking sports is only one small part of a healthy father and son relationship. Talking and listening to personal topics such as girlfriends, emotional ups and downs, sexuality, and ways to help others are essential. Talking about memories and past personal mistakes is another way to have a strong connection with a teenage son. Without all of these topics being a part of father and son communication, boys are set up to immaturely look elsewhere for such information and experiences or become too absorbed in superficial activities such as sports or games. Neither of these options, which are undertaken as a substitute for time with a father, is a formula for inner strength and maturity for our sons.

Growing boys between the ages of 7 and 11 begin looking up to their fathers as heroes. They believe their father knows everything and that whatever their father does, he does best. They easily exaggerate and make up stories about their father and his endeavors. This is done primarily because boys at this age are developing a self-image that needs to include masculinity. Love for their father and desperately

---

14   Haapasalo

trying to be just like him is a natural way to internally accomplish this developmental task.

Boys between the ages of 12 and 16 begin to view their father in more realistic ways. They see their dads as more human and notice some of their own personality differences. This dissipates the earlier hero worship stage, and if the father is consistent, available, and supportive of their differences, the boy's efforts to assimilate into their world are positively facilitated. Through both of these developmental phases, sons continually watch, listen, and learn from their father's words and actions. As P. Amato found in a 1986 study, "The degree of parental involvement with children and older adolescents is strongly related to their self-esteem."[15] Any emotional unavailability, personal topic avoidance, or discomfort with closeness is generally perceived by sons as a negative toward himself and internally held as self-blame and doubt. Many of the boys I see in therapy who do not have a healthy relationship with their fathers continually struggle among their peers in immature ways in order to compensate for the lost or empty feelings they experience from their own fathers.

Bill (12)

Jane brought her son Bill to therapy because his grades were going down, he had quit the swim team and she had received a high bill from the phone company for pornographic entertainment numbers. Bill dropped his head, while his mother continued talking. "He's just lazy. He sits around all day and plays his video games if I let him. He won't even talk to me anymore. He just gives me one word answers when I ask him questions."

"Life was better after his dad left, but now, after two years, Bill seems depressed. I don't know why it would affect him now. The hard part was all the tension and arguing before we separated." Their divorce had been finalized six months ago so his father could remarry, and Bill visited his father on weekends. With his brown eyes mostly looking down, Bill added, "It's boring with my dad. He's always busy and he's always crabby—especially toward her." His mother added, "He means his father's new wife. It used to be me, but no more."

---

15   P. Amato

I asked Bill when he and his mother have their fun. He looked at me and frowned. "What do you mean?" His mother could also not remember the last time the two of them had laughed together. When I asked more about his father, Bill went to one word answers and then slowly painted a picture of good memories of his father, but ever since the separation he said he had been different. They didn't talk much about anything and he never came to his swim meets. Seeing his dad on weekends used to be nice, but lately he was often left hanging out with his step-mom.

My more personal questions about the phone calls and sex revealed that Bill remembered having sex education in 5th grade. He never asked his mom or dad about sex, and he and his friends always told each other sexual jokes. As he talked, I could see sadness in his eyes when he answered questions about his dad, and a boyish spark when he talked about his friends and their jokes. He denied making some of the pornographic calls, saying his friend had also made a few. His mother began shaking her head and Bill reacted with silence. I suggested a session with his father.

His mother raised her eyebrows and said, "Fat chance."

Bill initially said, "I don't know," but then added, "if 'she' doesn't come with him."

Bill's loneliness for his father was growing, and it's effects were beginning to emotionally paralyze him. Without attention and involvement with his father, any therapy would likely prove fruitless. In his sadness, Bill was resorting to what many boys do: becoming preoccupied with something exciting, not only to distract, but to give some energy to his depression. The availability of sexually explicit material and its excitement is what attracts too many boys toward inappropriateness. The gaping loss of a close and open relationship with their fathers is what sets them up for inappropriate behavior, and re-connecting a son with his father is what can help them. Bill's choice of pornographic phone calls was not a coincidence. It conveniently directed his anger for a step-mom who took his father's attention away from him, and also possibly frustrations with his own mother. Bill's reactions are a common pattern for boys who are overly interested in inappropriate sexual material. They miss their father's time and attention and distracting their true emotions onto sex is convenient in our society.

Usually, fathers are unsure of how to connect personally as their sons become teenagers and therefore move further away from them. Instead of trying new activities or words, fathers tend to get busy with other things or preoccupied with following professional sports. Their sons can feel emotionally abandoned, which can lead to distracting themselves to pornography or disrespect toward their mothers.

In Bill's case, his father refused to attend appointments with his son, saying that his new wife did not approve. Bill's time in therapy proved to be long and hard, with many setbacks when his hopes were unmet again by a father who had already abandoned him in the divorce.

Sexual Harassment

Sexual harassment is a recent phenomenon, not because it is new, but because it is being reported more openly. In the past, many boys and men were raised to act in disrespectful or harassing ways, and girls and women were raised to just accept these behaviors. Currently, the basic patterns for sexual disrespect or harassment still exist. It begins when boys are young and their parents unconsciously allow them to take turns first, then do the chore or favor that requires strength, or accepting their reckless or wild behavior by laughing. This grooming continues when parents do not immediately give any consequence to their son for pushing or hitting his sister. This type of reinforcement—of parents looking the other way when brothers are being aggressive with their sisters—produces inappropriate behavioral differences in kids merely because of their sex.

This grooming process continues when parents do not expect boys to clean the bathroom, hold the baby, or help cook a dinner. This not only creates sibling tension and fighting, it also draws distinct lines between the sexes in an acrimonious way and makes it harder for them to work together.

The unconscious setting up continues into grade school when parents focus more time and importance on their sons' activities and sports than on their daughters', encouraging sons to be aggressive in order to win, or wrestling with sons but not with daughters. When kids experience these subtle attitudes and reinforced behavior patterns throughout their grade school years, it has a profound and lasting effect on their viewpoint of the sexes.

In middle school and junior high, these sexual differences are further reinforced when parents tell sons to take care of their mother while Dad is away on a trip, listening to their sons' opinions more than their daughters', and fathers giving priority to watching sports on television at the expense of just "hanging out"' and visiting with his daughter in her room. In high school, these differences are most noticeable when parents allow more freedom and later curfews for their sons, meeting their daughters' dates but not their sons', and high schools not having coed cheerleading squads. Although separately these subtle differences may not have a significant effect, cumulatively, they unconsciously create a pattern of negative sexual differences.

Although most boys will not engage in inappropriate and disrespectful behavior toward girls and women, too frequently boys do choose disrespectful sexualized behavior. Typically, it begins during middle school. A boy gets angry at a girl because she doesn't like him any more. He distracts and protects his hurt and embarrassment by teasing her. Soon his friends join with him and his teasing because some of them have also been rejected by a girl. The momentum builds when they are together in a group, and the teasing turns into loud razzing. Each boy tries to be funnier and more daring than the previous boy's comment. Their statements become more personally hurtful and degrading. One boy says she's fat. The next says she's fat because she's pregnant. And the next says she's pregnant because she does "it" with so many guys. The girl is hurt and tries to ignore what is happening to her. The boys are wild with laughter and in some situations, one or two of them will poke, pinch, or slap her buttocks. Even though they have already crossed appropriate verbal boundaries with their words, the inappropriate touching is extremely devastating to the girl. In middle school, a girl's most common response to being treated so negatively is to retreat and try to ignore it all so it will hopefully end more quickly. The boys walk away, knowing that what they did was wrong, but nobody does anything about it anyway. Their original feelings of hurt and embarrassment are securely covered up as long as they keep an intense focus on teasing girls.

These same boys continue the negative focus on girls when after school they all go over to one of the boy's homes to look at a sports magazine with pictures of women in revealing swimsuits. The women are all laid out and looking sexy. The boys make any kind of comment they want, and they all laugh at each other's words. As adults, we may not like the fact that our sons do such things, but parents don't really know what to do, so generally the boy's behavior is ignored. Quietly, many parents are hoping it is just a phase their son is going through and they sit back and continue watching the game on television—a game where young men are struggling for dominance on a field and a group of professional cheerleaders are dancing on the sidelines flaunting their bodies.

In our society there are simply too many experiences for boys and girls where these negative attitudes are played out and where any comments about these behaviors are withheld. The constant exposure presents and forms these negative attitudes and behaviors in our boys, and parental silence reinforces and strengthens the disrespectful momentum.

Some kids do get by without learning about sexuality from their parents; however, these kids often grow into young adulthood unprepared or undecided about many sexuality issues. They miss not being as close to their parents as they would have liked to have been, and they struggle with answers from others because their own upbringing did not lay the groundwork for self-assurance. Instead of creating kids who are comfortable asking questions, talking openly, and making informed decisions about sex, we have kids who merely react to what they see and hear. They are constantly trying to keep up with what everybody assumes they should know. This causes kids to reach outside of their homes and grope for all the information and experiences they can concerning sexuality. It may be because their parents were afraid or didn't know how to bring up the sexuality topic. It may stem from parents who were mesmerized by sexual entertainment, yet never respectfully discussed it, or from parents who were harboring or distracting themselves from some difficult or unresolved emotions concerning sexuality. The end result of these unbalanced and unopened parental stances has a cumulative effect on kids. The lack of openness passes from one generation to the next until nothing about sexuality is being communicated in respectful ways. This enables the media to not only have control, but gives it an absolute monopoly on the subject.

A glaring warning to us as parents is this: once the media has our teenagers, it is unlikely that we'll get them back. The years of fast-paced, sexually provocative glitz will habitualize them to society's attitudes and norms, and any periodic talks a parent tries to begin will not hold a candle to their media-produced and media-developed attention spans. It is the rare parent who can not only begin talks with a teenager, but also hold their attention with emotional excitement by sharing some of their own past personal experiences. Facts and figures bore most kids. The key is to talk personally, while keeping eye contact, or kids will internally fall asleep. The effects of our media are pervasive and convincing, and without parental input from a young age our kids don't have a chance at developing fully and maturely.

C.) The Ravaged

Unhealthy responses in our kids because of inappropriate exposure

Adults have abrogated their parental responsibility not so much by allowing their children and teenagers to view the media, but rather by not offering an alternative. In this scenario the media presentations become the norm. As a result, kids, seeing the media, hearing its messages talked about, and living within its reach have nothing to contrast it to. This strengthens its influence and keeps kids watching.

Children and teenagers need to assimilate their outside world and certainly the media is a part of all of our worlds. However, without a solid contrast, a complete and well-rounded perspective is difficult to reach. Parents who assume that their kids understand respect or that advertising doesn't make them do things are banking on personal wishes, and therefore an unpredictable risk. Our kids are simply bombarded too often for even a calm, yet essentially non-sexually talkative family atmosphere to have a true balancing effect. The calmness and respectful pace of a family is not the problem. The real problem is unspoken respect for sexual topics and not teaching a broader and deeper meaning of sexuality than the media.

It's important to note that the media doesn't act alone. Its effect is dependent on non-talking parents. It is this combination of media blitz plus parental non-talking that creates a narrow-minded crevice through which our kids fall. They have no contrast and no perspective in terms of frequent and open dialogue about sexuality. Therefore, they end up free falling into this chasm of narrowness that the media thrives on.

Although many teenagers' and children's behavior can be attributed to experimenting, identity-seeking rebelliousness, or to inner hurt and anger coming out sideways due to family problems or past victimization, their choice of sexual behavior as an outlet is unmistakably linked to their one-sided exposure to sex in our society. They see provocative clothing styles, and they want them. They repeat phrases and sexual innuendoes heard on the radio. They don't talk about sex in front of their parents, because their parents don't talk to them. They laugh and play off each other's looks and dress because that's how all are judged. And kids in therapy for inappropriate sexual actions cannot discuss personal questions without their talk being replete with incomplete and inaccurate sexual knowledge.

In a society that does not condone or practice open and respectful talk and actions surrounding sexuality and non-sexualized nudity, yet allows and protects advertisers who use provocative sexual messages and models, one can see that our kids' choices are just part of the accepted picture. Certainly some of their behavior is an exaggerated form of what they see, and it ought to be treated accordingly; however, kids seeing a behavior, imitating it, and taking it one step further is too common. The exaggeration is their responsibility. The ideas, the atmosphere, and the unintended pushing of kids to the threshold of inappropriateness are adults' responsibilities. Our children's and teenagers' comfort with this blatant and sexualized showiness of women and men has been carefully and constantly groomed by adults' acceptance of such sexual presentations and their silence surrounding anything different. When kids see or experience no other way, choosing negative behaviors within their current realm is understandable. However, merely understanding this pattern should not encourage acceptance. Adults in a society need to nurture and protect their children so the exaggeration line is not crossed. We need to actively invite our teenagers to back away from that inappropriate threshold we have so unknowingly pushed them up against.

This is accomplished by doing the opposite of what is currently happening: non-talk about sex, non-action about respectful nudity, and constantly viewing and acquiescing to the media's handling of sexuality. The alternative—of openly talking and then acting—is the most promising, because without it, the picture and reaction from our kids is bleak.

Unhealthy responses in our kids is due to inappropriate exposure to provocative sexuality and a lack of respectful family dialogue:

"She asked for it."

"Who cares? It was just a one night stand. Anyway, she can get an abortion."

"Oh, I hate that bitch. Why doesn't he notice me?"

"Mrs. Smith, I'm sorry to inform you that your 17-year-old son has been charged for being sexually active with a 14-year-old girl."

"You look sexier than her any day, so show a little more cleavage, girl, and get that boy."

"Oh, man! I've gotta get those jeans or no girl is going to look at me at the dance."

"Hey, did you do 'em?"

"Yeah, I boned her."

These are all surface statements—all sad, but all true. This is what too many teenagers sound like who are growing up in America today, and they learned it by watching and listening to an adult world that prioritizes sexual entertainment.

It's loud. It has a selfish, showy attitude to it and it is without appropriate adult influence. I am not referring to parental expectations on how their kids should act. I am referring to total absence of influence in sexually healthy ways. Children and teenagers who do not experience the closeness and influence of mature, adult sexuality talk and actions struggle to go deeper than the surface. They don't know how. No one has shown them. Instead, they become preoccupied with the advertising they hear and the showy presentations of the sex they see in movies, television, and music videos.

When this occurs, too often teenagers choose behavior that is not respectful. They become caught up in the excitement of being with their peers, and they imitate and react to what they are inundated with everyday. Respect lines get clouded by the hyperness of the moment and the limitless ideas they've been exposed to in the media. Boys keep talking with and teasing a new girl in a movie theater to the point of discomfort.

Girls call numerous times in one evening if the boy they like is home. Boys try to look cool and attempt to be in control. Girls try to look pretty and provocative and attempt to get a boy to notice and hopefully like her by playfully being submissive to him. They use foul language, and sexual slang becomes commonplace. Proper or respectful sexual words are not familiar, along with respect, when referring to body parts.

Certainly, teenagers have a phase where they joke and tease and play off of each other. The problem is never giving them the developmental tools of respectful openness in order to get through this phase. It's rather obvious that the media is made up of adults who are stuck in an earlier adolescent disrespect phase. Adults in the media business are always trying to look younger, sexier, and say the most clever lines to make fun of someone else. I believe the effect on our young people from constantly being exposed to disrespectful presentations not only entices them into remaining in this stage, but also encourages and manipulates them to act—out. Both effects are devastating to our young people's task of healthy and mature individual development.

Tommy (16)

When Tommy's mother brought him to the first appointment, she refused to come into my office.

"It's his problem. He needs to deal with it," she stated in a voice that revealed more fear than confidence.

"Don't worry about it," he shot back. "I'll deal with it."

He quickly walked into my office and requested that I shut the door. As he began to talk, I noticed that he had the same feigned confidence in his voice that his mother did. He was a tall, handsome young man, but he had a crook in his mouth when he talked that gave me the feeling he was covering something up.

"My mom, she's just weird. And I don't even know why the court ordered me here. What I did was stupid, but it was no big deal. The courts aren't going to teach me anything I don't already know." He kept looking right at me as he talked.

Apparently, he had been pinching his younger sister's butt and joking about her developing breasts. His mother heard him on one occasion and asked the school counselor for advice. The counselor appropriately brought it to the attention of social services. Tommy went on to say that his sister laughed the first time he did it. Later, she just pulled away and went to do something else, which made him think it was no big deal. Besides, he said, his older sister's boyfriend always did it to her and she didn't react at all. Sometimes he would watch late night television with his sister and her boyfriend, and they were usually under a blanket poking at each other. If she jumped or screamed they would laugh and then kiss each other.

His dad was a traveling salesman and his mother worked part time in day care. He could never remember having a family meeting, and usually his parents watched their own television upstairs. Tommy and his sisters had the downstairs television and it was their job to keep the room picked up.

"They don't come down that much, so it's no big deal if things were a mess."

Listening to Tommy, it was apparent that there were many things that bothered him, but he avoided them by labeling everything that happened around him as "no big deal."

Tommy's mother would only agree to come into my office if he moved to the waiting room. She was as talkative as Tommy and made it very clear that she never parented him in any way that would give him the idea to harass his sister. She was in charge of parenting the kids because of her husband's long work hours, but she had not raised Tommy to be that way. She didn't think it was her place to talk to Tommy about sex education, but she wasn't sure if her husband had talked with him. She had given her daughters a book to read, but they had no questions. "Maybe they learned enough in their school sex education classes," she stated.

She had seen books for boys on sex education, but she assumed that her husband would buy one and give it to Tommy. She said she would call me after asking her husband, because she didn't think he would talk to me. He had been embarrassed and angry about his son's behavior and thought it best to forget it and not talk about it. He was a good dad, taking Tommy hunting and fishing, but he left the talking up to her.

Because I recommended ongoing counseling, I eventually met Tommy's father and sisters. During one session his older sister said, "I knew he would get into trouble some day. He used to do the same things to me until I got a boyfriend. Now he leaves me alone."

Although his father showed his disapproval through head shaking and frowns, he was a man of few words. Unfortunately for his son, and combined with exposure to unhealthy sexual presentation, Tommy was being pushed into a world of sexual disrespect without appropriate preparation.

There are times when children and teenagers simply imitate what they see. In Tommy's case, he really only experienced sexuality in disrespectful or sneaky ways. Without open talks with adults to act as a guide, he did not develop age-appropriate maturity. In the absence of appropriate openness and healthy expression, he carried out his natural curiosities in a hurtful way. Getting caught up in his habit, he put himself and especially others at risk. His counseling program included family sessions, as well as group therapy with other boys his age. This approach assisted his necessary learning within his peer group in terms of social skills and friendship priorities. Another important aspect was a complete sex education series with his family. Not only did it open up the whole area of healthy sexuality and impart accurate information, it also gave words, practice, and time for the beginning of a closer father/son relationship.

Touching Too Soon

When children watch movies or television programs with provocative sexual content and notice the adult's discomfort around them, they become embarrassed, giddy, and learn to not talk about it. When teenagers watch

movies or television shows with provocative sexual content, they remember the images whenever they socialize with friends at a party. The constant and repetitive sexual provocativeness in the media builds a precedent to become sexual. Whether they are at a party or a friend's house, when they are with someone they are attracted to, there is an unspoken pressure to become sexual. In situations like these, over time, it is the rare teenager who will hold back sexually.

Although initially many teenagers will not go far sexually, the subtle pressure is present, and eventually too many teenagers succumb. The whole unwritten picture is one that leads them into sexually intimate touching before they really know what they're doing. Mentally and emotionally, they are in over their heads. They are engaging in words and actions they did not learn through respectful, age-appropriate openness and experiences. They've seen them on television, movies, and advertising, but they haven't had the chance to talk about them or see a different picture. As a result, they try to do whatever is possible regardless if they should. Without consistently open talks, they take on too much, too fast.

These teenagers will experience consequences for their actions through guilt, jumping relationships, not belonging to a group, or pregnancy. In the long term it will affect them because they have not developed the relationship skills to work through problems or difficult times. A majority of their lives have been influenced by sex in surface, or showy ways so they come to believe that sex will make everything all right. Sometimes it does, in the short term. But in the long term, love, within a caring relationship which includes listening, sharing tears, supporting each other's differences, and nurturing some independent growth in each other, is often not learned or is secondary to sex. Without a deep relationship, sex wears out and the relationship quickly becomes stagnant and unhappiness ensues.

Kari (17)

Kari was referred to therapy by her doctor for depression. Her doctor had prescribed medication, but she knew she needed more than just medicine. Kari had contracted herpes at the age of 16 and the bouts of pain and discomfort were taking a significant emotional toll. The biggest factor, Kari said, was what it had done to her social life.

"He ruined my life. Even my girlfriends hardly call anymore. If I call them it's fine, but I'm always getting in on things they've already planned—without me."

Her mother sat in tears and listened as her youngest daughter told yet another professional her story. She began slowly, but this young girl's strength grew as she talked. Her voice became louder, her words more confident.

She described what she thought was a normal life before "it" happened. Every weekend she would go out with her friends. Sometimes they would have plans and other times they would get together at someone's house and then decide what to do. They had fun, but she and her friends always wanted a boyfriend. "If you were hitched with some guy," she explained, "you had a ticket to every dance, football game, and party. And guys rule at our school."

Kari had not made the cheerleading team, but after all, it proved to be more fun hanging out behind the grandstand rather than in front of it. "Besides, as long as I was dating one of the jocks, it was okay."

Her mom spoke for the first time. "All of them seemed like such nice boys. I just couldn't believe it when she told me it was Chris. He was always so polite and friendly."

"Yeah, well he was with me, too," Kari said, "but to keep a guy like that you have to get intimate. I wasn't really comfortable at first, but everybody did it, so I just got used to it."

She shared that she really began liking him and kept her first outbreak a secret from him. "I thought maybe I had gotten it from somebody else, and I didn't want Chris to know. But then I realized that it had been three months that I was with Chris, so he must have been messing around on the side."

Apparently, Chris was cavalier when she confronted him and said it wasn't his fault. He had no idea the other girl had them. Breaking up with Chris was harder then Kari thought, but "I was so hurt and mad, I could-n't stand to look at him."

After the breakup, a lot of her time was taken up with doctors, reading about herpes, and trying different creams and ointments. "The only way I could go to the bathroom at first was sitting in a warm bath. It stung too much to go on the toilet."

Over the past year Kari explained that her herpes seemed to improve faster than the first few bouts. However, her social life was getting worse, and through tears she said, "Everybody knows, and I haven't even come close to having a boyfriend. I mean, how am I going to get a boyfriend after getting this curse?"

Kari talked more about her loneliness and fear of the future—how two of her friends had gotten pregnant and how even that was better than herpes. She wanted to get help, but nothing seemed to work out. Her mom and sisters were helpful, but always feeling sorry for her. Her mother sat, quietly shaking her head in disbelief.

Near the end of the session I referred Kari to a young women's group at a local teen clinic. She was going to need the honesty and support of her peers to deal with her issue. It was unfair what had happened to her because not only was she victimized by this boy, but she was also victimized previously by the pressure to become sexually active. This pressure and constant message is pervasive within the media, as well as in its extension into our teenager's lives.

Mature or Superficial

It is important to briefly examine this aspect of how teenagers are not learning the real skills of a mature relationship: the actual witnessing of the skills and ensuing maturity that get couples through hardships and difficult times. Some of these concrete skills of communication involve taking a turn listening, even when angry or in disagreement; supporting your partner, even when you would have done it differently; going slowly and sticking to the issue; taking short breaks rather than yelling and trying to bring the discussion to a quick end; and sitting back and allowing your partner to share an experience without interrupting or trying to fix it. Practiced over time and always relying on love to go forward, these are the skills that occur regularly in a deeply committed and mature relationship.

We would be hard-pressed to remember the last time we saw one of these relationship skills being acted out in a movie or television show, but it is exactly these skills and maturity level that create and maintain deep, personal relationships. Not sex. Not showy clothing. Not "me-centered attitudes" or "finger-pointing behavior."

In our society, we know that our children and teenagers have seen much of the sexual input and excitement of the short-term or new relationship, but very little exposure to the real building of a long-term relationship. They see a couple on television arguing and then one of them says a hurtful statement and leaves. This doesn't give them the impression that couples stay at it until it's resolved. On the contrary, it gives them the idea that when you're upset you simply drop a verbal bomb and leave your partner to stew about it. When they see movies, primarily made up of a man or woman leaving their spouse for another romantic relationship, they don't see people staying committed to each other. They see people following their current desires and going after what's new and exciting. Also, when they see adults obsessed with looking younger, losing weight, or accomplishing a great physical feat, they don't think age, experience and maturity are important. They begin to believe, like most adults, that their worth is in how they look.

There are numerous superficial, as well as serious, examples of children and teenagers who have gotten sexual messages, but not relationship messages. They include, but are not limited to, the time and energy spent on styles and looking good; the ever-present discomfort and embarrassment whenever sexual topics arise; teasing by parents when their children are attracted to someone of the opposite sex, and the pervasive American pat

tern of boys not being able to understand another's feelings or viewpoint, and girls believing that when things go wrong it is somehow their fault.

Too often, groups of boys in our society choose aggressive behaviors that physically or emotionally hurt others. Their victims are usually other males who are physically not as strong, or girls they are mad at or don't like anymore. Their loud laughter and preoccupation with the next activity hinders the recognizing of any feelings and keeps remorse at bay.

On the other side, girls are likely to become subservient to boys. They often act out their anger by gossiping with many girlfriends about another girl—or against themselves. This can take the form of eating disorders, social withdrawal or depression. Typically, under stress, girls have a tendency to emotionally retreat while boys usually engage in more outwardly aggressive behaviors towards others or sometimes even in the form of suicide.[16]

In our society, these subtle behavioral roles have consequences on our children, and especially on our teenagers. Many males act out sexually aggressive behaviors against females. This happens slowly over time as they are given attention and praise for their physical accomplishments and showing off. When this pattern is coupled with little or no healthy sex education and minimal regard for another person's feelings, disrespectful physical and sexual acting out becomes commonplace. Instead of actual experiences of helping someone else or understanding another's feelings and viewpoint, boys are taught and given credit for personal accomplishments. Too often these accomplishments are at the expense of other individuals.

Most often girls are looked upon favorably if they are nice, pretty, and quietly accept the control of boys. They have learned that to get attention and popularity they need to accentuate their legs, waist, buttocks, breasts, lips, eyes, hair and shapely figure. After a while, it becomes second nature and being looked over by boys becomes commonly accepted. The expectation that goes along with being pretty

16   National Center for Health Statistics

and nice is that if you look good and act nice, things will go well. When something happens that is scary or hurtful, many girls tend to be quiet and hold it inside. They fear that talking about it will show others that they did something wrong. This pattern is most noticed and reinforced when parents confront their teenage daughters for being present when something bad happens. The words, "Well, what were you doing alone with him in the first place?" ring in their ears too often to feel anything else but guilt.

When parents talk about their boys, the words and assumption is that there wasn't much we could do because he was on his own. It's almost like saying, "He's out of control when he's away from us." When boys hear, "Well, next time don't go out with her, or have someone else with you," what else can they think but that it's not their fault? It's "the situation" or "she led me on." Not only does this subtle mindset erode our daughters' independent strength, it gives boys the image and belief that they are only capable of reacting to stimuli. This message is so degrading it ought to be reserved for describing robots, not people.

Too often parents, in their discomfort, avoid expressing their feelings and go directly to what could have prevented the situation rather than what really happened. For example, instead of saying, "I can't believe you did something so mean to her," parents often say, "Well, be careful next time or you'll really get into trouble." This response avoids the main point. The truth is, someone was vulnerable and someone took advantage. That's wrong, no matter what the circumstances. Focusing on the circumstances first is a very subtle way that parents inadvertently promote the societal roles that boys acting out is expected and that girls are guilty for being there.

Many teenagers are ravaged by these subtle gender roles and confusion about sex. Our society has victims of sexual abuse, victims of incessant teasing and ridicule and victims of their own body types. They are made to feel that way by the messages of perfection viewed in advertising and the media. This so-called perfect body image is subtly supported by all adults who do not talk about or present a different way.

Terry (17)

When the tall, blonde-haired Terry walked into my office, he lit up my waiting room with his smile. He had a naïve attentiveness to him that almost made him look vulnerable. If I hadn't read the intake sheet, I would have judged him to be the victim. However, it was Terry who had been charged with sexually aggressive behavior.

On the weekend after school let out, several of his friends told him about a pick-up party. There was going to be a huge bonfire and several area high schools knew about it. As Terry said, "Everybody was going to just let loose and celebrate summer vacation." It was called a pick-up party by his friends because there would be a lot of girls they didn't know. If all went well, they would each leave the party with one of them.

Terry explained that he was open to meeting new girls because he had-n't had a girlfriend since the winter quarter. Because the young man having the party obtained a fire permit, he warned everyone not to bring alcohol. He was sure the police would check on them due to the size of the fire. This didn't bother Terry because, "I'm not a big drinker, but I did-n't want to take any chances on getting a ticket because it would be my third one this year."

With confidence he told me about his family and his job. He was the oldest of four, but the two babies were from his dad's new marriage. He got along with his dad, but despised his step-mom. "She's always telling my dad what I should and shouldn't be doing." Also, his 14-year-old sister usually followed him around if his friends came over to hang out. "That bugs me, but I let her or my dad will get mad at me."

His speech became noticeably shaky as he answered questions about his behavior.

"We were all just goofing around at the party and I could tell this one girl liked me. She kept pushing me toward the fire and laughed whenever I said anything. Some of my friends said I better take her for a ride before she loses interest."

At that point Terry said he left the party and took her for a ride in his car.

"We didn't talk much once we got in the car. I turned the radio up and asked her to sit next to me. When she did, I automatically put my arm around her. She kind of leaned into me, so I put my hand down her shirt."

He began shaking his head as he told me the rest of his story.

"She said 'don't' but didn't move away from me, so I figured it was okay to keep trying. I started to rub underneath her bra and she said 'please stop' and reached for my hand. I suppose I got a little carried away because I kept touching her and pulling her closer. I thought she would just relax, but she didn't."

Terry went on to say that eventually the girl did pull away from him. He attempted to comfort her, but at a stop sign she jumped out of his car.

"I got out to tell her it was okay and I'd bring her back to the party, but I got scared when she ran up to somebody's house. She was crying, so I got out of there."

Two weeks later the police came to Terry's door to interview him about the incident.

"I thought the whole thing was over and done with until these two cops came to my house. I didn't admit to it at first because my step-mom was there. Later, when I appeared in court, I did admit it."

Although Terry was open and talkative with all my questions, it was apparent that he really didn't understand why the police got involved or his appearance in court. It seemed to him that everybody else was trying to pick up a girl, and for once he had gotten lucky. He also focused on surface issues rather than what he had really done. He wondered how she could report him because he didn't remember exchanging names. He did-n't know why she just didn't call him and demand an apology, and he was hoping that news of the incident would not become public.

He would have much work to do in therapy. Initially, he was angry with me for requiring his whole family to attend sessions. However, without complete openness on personal topics like sexuality, anger within his family, and appropriate personal boundaries, he would not have a chance to remorsefully resolve his inappropriate behavior and responsibly understand it. Many kids in Terry's situation are too accustomed to moving forward quickly and on the surface when sexualized things occur. Our fast-paced, provocative media trains them well for moving on without regrets.

Victims

There are many subtle aspects to the pervasive blaming of victims in our society. Often, people's first reaction to someone who says they have been verbally offended is defensiveness. Someone explains that a label or joke makes them feel put down, and people who have laughed will say, "Oh, come on, loosen up; he didn't mean anything by it."

This response is subtle, but the message is clear. Get over it, or ignore it, but let us have some fun with you. In 1994 a speaker at a public forum was telling jokes that made fun of a particular ethnic group. Later, when someone in the audience asked about his inclination for telling such jokes, he defensively said, "I think we are all becoming too thin-skinned." I remember thinking, *now there's a person who's supporting some of our cold societal attitudes.* His words were saying "It's not his fault for telling the ethnic jokes, but the people of his jokes for being too thinned-skinned." It was a blatant statement defending his selfish habit of making fun of others. I can say what I want and if someone gets upset, then it's their problem for being too sensitive.

We must remember that victims speak to something wrong in a society. They have been discounted as an individual or a group, and their courage to speak-out indicates a need for change. If a person or society responds with defensiveness or further discounting, the chance for change and compromising for the benefit of both has been lost. In such a society, victim numbers increase and strong cohesive growth as a group is severely hindered. Instead of compromising and moving forward together, sides are taken and a fight is imminent.

Pushing the Sexualized Step

Unchecked media-viewing without parental dialogue sets up kids to believe that sex is behind everything. They begin feeling that the finest thing anyone can do is have sex, touch the opposite sex's body, or have someone touch their own body. This message—although subtle and somewhat disguised—comes through loud and clear for kids who don't have a place to talk openly about sex. When they see sexually suggestive advertising in everything from cars to lipstick, perfume, and clothes they are filled with wonder and excitement—wonder about the models in the presentation and their loosely covered bodies, excitement about the possibility of sexually touching such a body, and fantasizing about actually being in a relationship with the model. It has nothing to do with the product being advertised, but everything to do with viewing the models in a sexual way. Unexpressed in healthy ways, these constant sexualized presentations contribute to kids' internal energies, and therefore are just waiting to be expressed. Too often this expression comes out in jokes or making fun of someone in a sexual way. Thinking about the sexually-presented models in advertising and fantasizing about the next sexual step can become a preoccupation with teenagers who view it and have no place to talk about it.

This next suggested sexual step by the media is where its influence lies: children and teenagers who really don't know what that next step is. They usually don't have caring experiences in sexual intimacy, so they are held by the visuals of red lips, pants slipping down, and hair flying, all shown in high speed flashes and dubbed over with provocative music. This appeal holds their attention and keeps them thinking and fantasizing about what they've seen. If teenagers don't have avenues to talk about sex in respectful ways and view caring, non-sexual nudity, the presentation invites them to act in the same non-caring ways. Some kids change relationships quickly after becoming sexually intimate, others become sexually and verbally harassing, while others hold it all inside and privately become habitualized to pornography. All of these behaviors are personally destructive, but they have nowhere else to go with their energies and curiosities in our closed-mouth society.

Older to Younger

Acting out in a sexually provocative manner or showing only a loose, exciting side of sex to young teenagers who don't know much about sexuality is extremely selfish and one-sided. This happens every time our kids watch the majority of their favorite musical groups or individuals. These individual singers or groups are dancing in front of an audience of kids not even half their age. They are showing kids something they know little about and have little personal experience with. It holds their attention and fills their minds with exciting, bigger-than-life images.

Their provocative antics are similar to a 12-year-old showing a fouryear-old a piece of candy they've stolen. Absolutely gripping and mesmerizing for the four-year-old, but only because it's so new and different. However, when a four-year-old can be shown what stealing is, its consequences, what the opposite is, and be allowed to talk about it and play it out, they have a removed interest in the 12-year-old and the bragging. It is a similar parallel for children and sex. If they have an adult they can talk about it with, see in pictures or movies how it can happen respectfully, and have chances to see unclothed human bodies in non-sexual ways, they are also removed emotionally from the showiness of their musical artists. This is where their maturity develops because they have a different and deeper personal experience of sexuality than the shallow media presents.

If children and teenagers do not have an appropriate outlet for expressing their sexual curiosities, asking questions, or learning more about bodies, caring intimate touch, and non-sexual nudity, they will likely act out their energies and drive to learn in immature ways. Our society is filled with behavioral examples of out of context, immature actions on the part of unknowing and naïve children and teenagers. Sexual joking and sexual harassment are extremely prevalent. Coyish behavior on the part of girls and aggressive behavior on the part of boys abound. Teasing someone who's not as big and strong as the other boys or not as pretty and well developed as the rest of the girls is evident. Some of these patterns create ravaged teenagers because they have lost out on important socialization. For example, teenage girls try for years to look pretty. They do all the make-up. They make sure they have the newest styles of clothes. When many are not asked out on a date, they feel crushed. They believe they are not as good as other girls who supposedly look prettier. Not only are they ravaged because they're fighting low self-esteem, but they feel like they've missed something. And they have.

Many girls have missed years of fun doing boy/girl social activities because of the distraction of who's better because she's prettier, or has bigger breasts, or a nicer butt in certain jeans. They have actually bypassed important group and peer socialization activities—even the chance to go out and have fun at a drive-in restaurant without concern over who ate the most or going to a movie and not worrying about how she looks when she laughs. These sorts of experiences with other peers build character, self-esteem, and a sense of belonging, all prerequisites to successful personal relationships and long-term happiness. But the pressure and drive to look pretty and be perfect destroys too many of the opportunities for levelheaded, age-appropriate fun and therefore complete social development.

Teenage boys do not escape adolescence without being ravaged either. Their pressure and drive to be cool, funny and in control hinders the majority of their emotional development. When they are more concerned about what cologne to use rather than inviting a new boy to join in, they are too lost in image to recognize a feeling. When they are more focused on being or looking the strongest, they are too shallow to see the right thing to do when someone is hurt. When they are thinking more about making the next joke at someone else's expense, they are too preoccupied to even hear another's invitation for meaningful communication. These patterns tune boys out to their intuition and emotions and keep them attuned to other boys' surface behaviors and superficial banter to find belongingness and inclusion. Their outward, competitive focus is not a good predictor of being emotionally open and honest in their personal relationships.

Keith (17)

Keith walked into my office like a tired football player. He was husky and swayed side to side as he carried his bulk through my now seemingly small doorframe. He said he came alone because he didn't want to embarrass his parents any further. A senior in high school, he had been driving for almost two years. Soon he would have enough money for his own car. But, he told me that's where the problem was. Instead of using his savings account on a car, he had to pay a court fine and a victim's counseling fee.

With indignation in his eyes, he told me that "those dumb-ass cheerleaders told on us. It was just a stupid game that they started and when it got to be too much, they freaked and told the coach."

Apparently, Keith and the rest of his wrestling team were staying in a downtown hotel for the state championships. On the second night, several cheerleaders came to the team's room to hang out. They had completed their matches and would be spectators the rest of the weekend. One thing led to another, he said, and eventually two of the cheerleaders were trying, in fun, to wrestle him down. He bragged that he quickly pinned both of them down and his roommates, seeing the girls in such awkward positions, began pinching them. The pinching turned into tickling, and the tickling turned into "copping a feel." The girls' laughs turned to screams, and then tears. "When they started crying I let them up, but before that it was all in fun," he stated.

I asked Keith if he had ever been in a situation where it was supposed to be fun but that it didn't feel fun to him. At first he answered, "No," but then he stared out the window. His eyes began to mist over and I invited him to say more.

"In 7th grade I was one of the last guys in my grade to mature. Whenever we had gym class, the instructor made us take showers before changing back into our regular clothes. I was called 'baldy,' 'hairless wonder,' and 'baby head boy.'" He struggled to continue and said his classmates laughed, tried to snap him with their towels, and joked about him in the hallways. It wasn't until 10th or 11th grade that he got some respect back for being on the wrestling team. He looked back at me and said, "I never told anybody this before, because I had to act like I didn't care."

Keith was devastated back in 7th grade when that happened to him, and he was devastated now. Until I treated his own victimization and helped him heal, he would be emotionally unable to understand what he had done to the cheerleaders. He agreed to further appointments after I assured him that what he said would remain confidential.

In Keith's situation, he was similar to many boys and young men in our society. He did what was done to him. The actual behavior was different, but it was sexual, and he made his victims feel powerless. When it happened to him, he was sexually embarrassed and felt powerless to stop it. Not only do sexually offensive things happen to boys, but most of them bury it deep inside and don't talk about it. As a result, it often comes out years later in their own insensitive behavior toward someone else. Most of the boys and young men I see in therapy for inappropriate sexual behavior need to also resolve themselves being victimized at some point in their lives. Sexual embarrassment, harassment, and abuse is common among kids in our society. Much of it goes unreported, and therefore shows up routinely when males are in therapy for current behavior problems. Our society does not protect kids very well, therefore the cycles of abuse continue.

A common habit in parents who are caught up in day-to-day busy schedules is to wait until their children or teenagers bring up sex education questions. These parents provide well for their children, involve them in numerous after-school activities, and do family outings on weekends. Everyone appears happy, so the knack or habit of talking about personal topics is never developed or given a place within the family. However, parents allow television, videos, and the Internet into their homes. Feeling safe because these transmissions are in their own homes, they use them and comfortably let their kids use them. Our society's sexually provocative messages find their way even in these media services and therefore pollute even the privacy of our homes. Soon children and teenagers are repeatedly bombarded with sexual messages. They have no place for open sexuality talks or respectful depictions of the human body to counter what they're getting from all the media angles. The negative equation plays itself out again: numerous inescapable messages of sexually unhealthy images hitting their senses; no healthy talks or depiction of caring affection; and therefore, naïve or inappropriate behavior ensues, all in an attempt to understand what they're feeling, seeing, and partially learning. These are kids who need healthy and respectful sexuality talk, but instead they are closed off to it and hear none at all. The disrespectful sexual messages in our society are too pervasive to escape. It would require insurmountable amounts of time and energy to filter it all out. We know that sexuality is an integral part of the human psyche and therefore needs expression. The problem is that the media has taken over as the presenter of such information. Its self-appointed control of the subject has been buttressed by the silence of parents and adults who avoid the topic in most life areas of our children and teenagers. The solution is for parents and families to get back in the business of expressing and dealing with sexuality; however, it needs to be done more openly and more completely than the media.

Ellen (11)

Ellen came to my office with her parents after appearing in court. She had been charged with criminal sexual misconduct in the 4th degree. Ellen was 11 years old at the time. She was babysitting a 5-year-old boy, and while she was changing his clothes into his pajamas, she tried to make his penis get hard by pulling it. She kept trying until he said it hurt. Immediately, Ellen stopped what she was doing and read him a bedtime story.

The next day the police knocked at Ellen's house. The boy had told his mother that his penis was red because Ellen was pulling on it. Ellen denied she had done anything during the first five minutes of the interview. As the questions continued, she couldn't hold back her guilt. She admitted to the behavior, and her mother said she cried herself to sleep that night.

Two weeks later she appeared in court and was ordered to undergo a sexuality assessment. In my office, Ellen and her parents appeared worried, yet polite and talkative. They avoided saying too much about the behavior because Ellen would begin to cry. In order to ease the tension, I had them talk about other aspects of their lives. They were living in a small community, both parents enjoyed their jobs, and Ellen was attending the private school next to their church. She was involved in after-school sports, and she maintained a B average. They said Ellen had a nice group of friends and enjoyed doing sleepovers. She also enjoyed Sunday family nights because they played her favorite board games, and it was fun to have her older sister around.

As they became comfortable, I asked more personal questions. Although Ellen's smile left her countenance, she answered with dignity. She couldn't remember ever having sex education, and although one of her friends had started her period, she was waiting for her mother to tell her about it. Her mother thought it was best to wait until Ellen began asking questions. Her dad said Ellen was the quiet one, and he wasn't surprised that she hadn't asked any sex-type questions. Ellen's face became red and she had trouble looking up.

Ellen's sister piped up and said it was just like the pictures on the computer. Apparently, Ellen and her sister were playing on the computer one day after school and a pornographic service invited them into a program. The girls followed the instructions and within minutes had numerous pictures on the screen. They saw pictures depicting men and women in unusual poses and pulling at each other's private parts. There was no sound, but the pictures held their attention until they heard the garage door open. They turned off the computer before their mom walked into the house from work. The girls said they watched the pornographic service on their computer several days after school each week. One month after first viewing the pornographic pictures, Ellen was babysitting and did her behavior.

Ellen's parents were not aware of the computer service and resolved to cancel it. They also felt embarrassed for not having had sex education talks with their girls. Ellen's older sister said she had already learned about sex education in school and didn't need any more. Ellen was scared and visibly upset about doing something she never even imagined. Initially, therapy was uncomfortable for her family due to talking openly and completely about sexuality education topics. However, in time their communication skills improved and they developed a comfortable closeness. Ellen's victim was a resilient healer in his short-term therapy, and when the time was appropriate, Ellen, with both of her parents' support, made a sincere and emotional apology. Although her therapy was complete, Ellen would probably never forget what she had done, due to her negative exposure to sex without the voices of her parents for help.

Pornography

Children and teenagers cannot be exposed to adult pornography and its emotional effects and walk away unscathed. When they see adults, maybe even their parents, involved in viewing pornography, they become curious. As they follow their curiosities and seek more exposure, momentum builds and they become more habitualized and drawn to it. It gives them experiences in a world where nude bodies, sex, and turn-ons are depicted in non-caring ways. The focus is very much on the primitive sounds of groaning, coarse or rough fondling of private parts, and the absolute self-indulgent viewpoint of having an orgasm.

If kids witness this, not only can they become similar in focus and interest, but they also become emotionally flat and shallow. A part of their spirit is turned off and their energy for life begins to fade. To raise kids with this kind of exposure is a travesty because it does not instill a deep spirit or a passion for life. It does not teach them how to work with and get along with others and it does not demonstrate a priority for helping others that are less fortunate. Instead, it takes a very narrow focus of life and promotes a self-indulgence that thwarts emotional development.

Unfortunately, the sexually provocative nature of our media is more similar to pornography than it is different from it. It keeps the focus on people's private parts, it attempts to turn on those viewing it in a sexual way, and it demonstrates how to use sex to get what you want. The individual is presented as only someone or something special because they're flaunting their sexuality.

Although in my practice I've observed that kids who view our media are not as emotionally flat or depressed as kids exposed to pornography, they are primarily self-centered. Without a healthy contrast, including caring experiences with others, our kids are set up to find purpose in superficial and showy presentations. They have no concrete ground to stand on to judge what they see around them if adults and parents don't show them a deeper difference.

Jon (14)

When Jon entered my office, I was greeted with a naïve, boyish face in a linebacker's body. He was big and muscular for his age, but his face gave away his immaturity. His mother and father both attended the first appointment and each respectfully allowed Jon to speak for himself. As Jon's story unfolded, I began to realize why he looked so young, in spite of his bulk. At the age of 8, over the course of a year, he had been sexually harassed and abused by one of his older brother's friends. When his brother had friends over to play video games or watch movies, sometimes one of the friends would find Jon. At first this 13-year-old boy just teased and wrestled around. Soon it turned into pinching and hurting Jon's nipples. On one occasion Jon said he turned down an invitation to swim with a friend because his chest was bruised. He felt embarrassed and didn't want to tell his folks and get his brother's friend into trouble.

"My mom and dad really liked this friend of my brother's because he was friendly and talkative with me. I figured it was just a thing—you know, teasing your friend's younger brother—and soon it would stop."

But it didn't. After dinner one evening the boy came into Jon's room while the other boys were playing a video game.

"He walked in with this carrot and he was touching it in a funny way. And then it happened." Jon talked softer, yet kept going even while his mother began to cry. "He made me do it to his penis the way he was touching the carrot. I was so scared, I couldn't do anything else."

The boy's behavior went on for several months and Jon added that the boy started treating him nicer. "He wasn't so mean to me and didn't hurt my chest anymore. He acted like he was my buddy, but whenever I heard he was coming over I asked to go to a friend's house."

As time went on, Jon became adept at avoiding his brother's friend. He would go outside, call a friend over, or simply follow his mother or father around the house. The situation happened less often, but on one occasion, shortly after Jon's 9th birthday, his father walked into Jon's bedroom and saw him crying. His father spoke up. "He hugged me and wouldn't let go."

Jon's parents put an end to the boy's behavior. He was never allowed in their home again and they notified the boy's parents. Jon saw a counselor for 3 appointments and it was felt that as long as the behavior had stopped he would be all right.

Four years later, sexual problems hit Jon and his family again. This time it was Jon doing the behavior, and this time he was court ordered to my therapy program. On several occasions in the past year Jon had been playing with his grade-school aged cousins and had manipulated them with candy to touch his penis. His folks were shaking their heads and lamenting, "We should have known. We should have gotten more help for him back when it happened to him."

With tears in his eyes, Jon was as surprised as he was guilty. "I never wanted to scare anybody like what happened to me. I didn't even think; it just kind of happened."

Jon mentioned that he wanted to say he was sorry, but the court had ordered him to stay away from his victims. I informed Jon that not only did his victims need time for their own healing, but that he had much work to do in therapy before he could sincerely and completely apologize. Whether his victims could forgive him or even wanted to hear his apology was another issue to be decided later. For now, Jon would have to engage himself in the therapy program and do his personal work even before having the opportunity to apologize to his victims. Jon's therapy would be lengthy, because his own victimization needed healing prior to him being able to fully understand and change his victimizing behavior.

His parents were supportive of his involvement in the therapy program and attended regularly with him. Two years after beginning therapy, Jon successfully completed the program. He had openly healed many of his abused feelings, confronted his own negative compensating behaviors, and then was given the opportunity for an apology session by his resilient and forgiving cousins.

Eight months after his completion date, Jon contacted me to ask for support and advice. He had been asked to attend and give testimony at a court hearing regarding his brother's friend. Apparently his abuser was an adult now and had been caught abusing other younger boys. Jon had not seen or heard about his abuser in over 7 years. Keeping inside all the fear and anger of when he was 8 years old, he testified in a courtroom where his abuser sat listening. Although Jon said he was shaking on the inside, his folks said he seemed calm and spoke clearly as he gave his statement. Two weeks later, Jon was given word that his abuser refused to admit to his behavior and was sent directly to prison.

Later Jon said, "I think if I could have confronted him when I was younger, I would have never turned into one like him." I reminded Jon that although his behavior was similar, he was not like his abuser. He had admitted to it, attended therapy, and apologized for his mistake, things his abuser never came close to doing. With tears of newfound strength and relief, Jon said, "I still feel bad for what I did, but I'm glad I got better and changed."

It is estimated that approximately 22% of boys under 18 years of age have experienced some form of sexual abuse. The majority goes unreported. The estimation for girls under 18 is almost three times higher than that for boys. These behaviors are all happening in a society where sex is not talked about frequently in open and respectful ways, where fewer than 5% of our kids experience non-sexual, casual changing of clothes within their families, and where the media has an iron-clad grip on what and how sexual things are presented to our children and teenagers.

Parents who do not comment and bring up sexual topics are actually acquiescing to the presentations of radio disc jockeys, television programming, and advertisers' slanted view of bodies, sex, and relationships. The media does not, and cannot, develop or enhance strong personalities in our kids. Only parents can create the open atmosphere on important life topics, including sexuality, where kids can really learn and mature into strong personalities. Strong personalities are what give kids the ability to navigate and keep in perspective our society's negative presentation of sex, narrow male and female roles, and shallow relationship models.

2.) The Solution: Respectful Sexual Openness

A.) The Openness

Taking a Stand and Talking About It

The solution to this travesty, which has been put on our children and teenagers by the media and by adults avoiding the issue, is within our grasp. Although this solution is fairly straightforward and simple, it will be personally challenging because we as Americans are not accustomed to individual openness and taking positive personal risks. We have been lulled into passively watching actors and actresses portray the open and emotional part of life for us. They expertly play out personal human emotions and experiences while we sit back and watch. We become habitually captivated by what we see. It is in this constant captivation that our gumption and incentive for change is eroded. In order to reclaim our personal energies and efforts, we need to seriously limit media exposure and begin practicing open talks, and eventually actions, with our spouses, children, and friends.

Taking a Stand by Talking and Doing.

Complete openness is the answer. This complete openness has two sides to it. The first is complete openness in our talk about sexuality and sex questions—of any type—with our children and teenagers.

The second is complete openness in our actions, which means having respectful pictures and books on sexuality available, as well as casual non-sexual family nudity. These actions need to be in appropriate places, like stepping from the bathroom to the bedroom, or changing clothes with doors open, or even skinny-dipping on a private family camping trip. In the first aspect of talking parents must initiate, invite, and listen without pushing the sexual topic or putting kids on the spot by asking a lot of questions. In the second aspect of actions, parents must comfortably enact and lightly have situations and experiences happen without forcing or making fun of their kids who don't participate. The important point is this: parents need to do it first. Kids will either slowly join in or ignore it, but at least both reactions will give kids an experience of healthiness whether they actually join in or not. Younger kids will join in, older kids may not; however, as long as parents sporadically show bodily comfort their kids have at least witnessed and experienced healthy body acceptance in non-sexual ways. Even if kids have only a few experiences of casual family nudity when they are grade school age or younger, it is enough to help put nudity and body acceptance into perspective. Ongoing, casual family nudity when kids become teenagers should only continue if all family members are comfortable. It can still be appropriate and comfortable, but again, it should not be made an issue; it should be done because all are comfortable and it happens naturally, otherwise keep your clothes on and your doors closed. The important message of healthy and respectful sexuality will only come across if adults are truly comfortable with their own words and actions. Therefore, adults and parents ought to take it one step at a time. With the help of practicing open talks with one's spouse or other adults, it becomes easier to talk with kids. Talking and doing only what is comfortable is the key to healthy and appropriate family interaction.

When children and teenagers are taught verbally and through adults' actions—a healthy, complete approach to sex and sexuality— they have no interest or use for tricky, unhealthy, sexually provocative messages in the media. It comes across as nothing but silliness to them. Uninteresting. Immature. Below their knowledge base. Because of this complete education to a healthy sexuality and some exposure to non-sexual unclothed bodies, the advertisers' trump card of enticing interest by trying to show something that kids don't know about or haven't seen is powerless. What the media uses to capture kids' attention is already talked about, asked about, and experienced so openly and respectfully that they are beyond the games and teasing of the media. To raise kids beyond what advertisers and the media choose to represent is instilling an incredible amount of power, choice, and maturity. To parent beyond the media in this healthy, open way is to be in charge—not by holding kids back from seeing sexuality, but by going beyond what the media shows them, although in healthy, caring, and respectful ways.

A child or teenager who has experienced open sexuality and knows that they can ask about or talk about anything they encounter in the media is a calm, confident individual. When they feel comfortable enough to actually walk away from the television, ask about a certain sexy commercial, and get a respectfully open answer, then comfort, knowledge, and a sense of power is gained. It also gives them a sense of choice, because they have the broader scope of real-life experiences and education, rather than the very limited and narrow viewpoint the media gives them.

Abstaining from sexual relations as a teenager is emotionally healthy. Abstaining from talking about sex and seeing or experiencing some non-sexualized nudity is not emotionally healthy. Many parents attend a school-sponsored sex education class with their child and rarely talk about the topic again. They often believe their children are not that interested because they tell their parents they have no questions or they change the subject. Parents incorrectly interpret this as non-interest or that their kids have enough knowledge of sexual topics. It should be interpreted as, "Hey, I'm uncomfortable too. Can we go a little slower?"

One of the positive things a parent can do is weave in and out of sexual topics, Sometimes lightly—in one or two sentences, other times more in-depth and personal. The key for parents is to stop putting their kids on the spot by asking them all the questions. It is more equitable and comfortable if a parent expresses their own feelings about a question first and then asks their child or teenager the same question. If the child or teenager answers or talks about the topic, parents have a dialogue. If there is no response or changing of the subject, the parent has to wait for another time.

A parent may begin a sexual topic conversation as follows:

"Seeing that sex education film tonight reminded me of when I first learned about sex The one thing they never told us much about was the girl's body and how it works, so it was fascinating to hear about that tonight. How about you, son? Was some of that new to you?"

"Yeah, I didn't know about all that stuff either."

If the conversation ended at this point by going onto other topics, that would be fine. If it went on, it may go this way:

"The thing I found most interesting was how that egg makes its way to the uterus. How about you? What did you think of that?"

"I don't know."

"Really?"

"Yeah, I thought it was more interesting how it fills with blood every month."

"Yeah, that's amazing, too, and then how it flows out when it knows there's no baby starting."

Again, the conversation could end there and that would be fine. If it did go on because the son was in a talkative mood, it might go like this:

"Dad, is it hard for girls to use those things they stick inside of themselves to get the blood?"

"That's a good question, but I've heard if they put the tampon into their vagina slowly it's okay. I think that would be a good question to ask Mom when we get home."

"Yeah, but it might embarrass her."

"Yeah, well let's ask her first if it's okay to ask a question about using tampons, because you're right, we always want to be nice, or, you know, respectful about personal topics. When you and your friends talk about personal stuff or sex questions, are they usually respectful?"

"Mmm, kind of. We usually don't talk about it, though, and never with the girls."

"Oh, do you think it might be talked about more now because of this family sex education class tonight?"

"Maybe, but now we know things, so we don't really need to."

"Mmm, well it's sure nice to be able to talk about these kinds of things with you, son."

"Uh-huh."

The father comfortably kept the conversation going, never focusing more than one question at a time on his son, sharing his feelings first, and not giving lectures on life. He even ended it with a compliment for what had just taken place between him and his son, rather than a future directive like "I hope you can always talk to me if you have questions." That message is implied in the compliment and in the positive and open way the father related to his son. Also, this father appropriately knows that he is more responsible for bringing up sex topics than his son.

The complete verbal and pictorial experiencing of sexuality and the multitude of human body types is the most powerful protector against the media, as well as the primary developer of sexual maturity. Without sexual talk being commonplace and comfortable, children and teenagers have gaps in their curiosities and knowledge base. As with all humans seeking information, these gaps can be quickly filled with mass media fads, advertising attitudes, and superficial or one-sided sexual opinions. Kids who have had the opportunity and experience of frequent sexuality talks, viewing pictures of non-sexual unclothed bodies of all sizes and shapes, and pictures of caring intimate sex as they grow older are filled with respectful, personal, caring images of sex and sexuality. They are caringly brought into the knowledge and respectful experience of the human body, as well as healthy and intimate touch in such a profound way that there is no room for silliness, superficiality, or narrow-minded depictions. The media and artificial intent of advertising in sexually provocative ways is lost in the experienced children and teenagers' maturity due to complete and respectful openness with their parents. Although experienced kids remain exposed to our mass media, its effect is unable to get a grip on their broader knowledge base.

Expecting Respect

When children and teenagers constantly experience and live with respectful sexuality talk and where any exposure to intimate sexuality is only through caring pictures, they will expect nothing less from within their own relationships. It is a habit of experience and acceptance that what kids are exposed to in their family relationships is exactly what they will tolerate or create in their own outside relationships. Unfortunately, kids who are raised in disrespectful family relationships are most likely to tolerate disrespect in their own life relationships.

However, kids raised respectfully gravitate toward similar respect in their life relationships and this positive pattern will repeat itself in their friendships. Sexual respect and caring must be experienced openly because it doesn't express itself naturally when kids have been raised in our negative, sexually provocative society. Taking back the responsibility of respectfully talking about sexuality and making available caring pictures of unclothed bodies and some sexual intimacy is the only tool for countering our society's negative picture of sexuality and developing true maturity in our children and teenagers.

Occasionally, younger kids feel comfortable talking or asking about sex; however, by the time kids are in grade school they know the topic is anxiously charged and it's better to keep quiet. Many kids in grade school will even hide their faces when the topic comes up or when they see couples in public or on television appropriately being affectionate or kissing. Their reactions are a clear indicator of media poisoning and lack of family openness. They experience nothing respectful or healthy about sexuality in their families, so they react exactly how the media has taught them to act.

Seeing grade school age children react with embarrassment sometimes looks cute or endearing. However, when we realize that this reaction is the culmination of years of being exposed to sex in only seductive or provocative ways, it takes on a different aspect. It's also important to remember that too often childhood embarrassment can turn into teenage rebellion in sexually permissive ways. If kids don't experience open sexuality while growing up, they will vicariously meet their need for sexuality openness through the media or in their own experimenting or rebellious behavior. Facts and statistics used to caution teenagers are merely numbers or words. They need real experiences and positive emotions surrounding family sexual openness in order to really learn, and therefore avoid the narrow-minded pitfalls of the media. Words will only stay in their heads. Positive emotions will carry them through life. As parents, it is imperative to ensure family talks are fun and the viewing of healthy sexual pictures is completely open.

Kids who have been raised in sexually disrespectful environments, even in subtle ways, are often terrified of the entire topic. Parents who don't know what to do, or themselves are uncomfortable with the topic, usually just let it go. They don't deal with it because they are overwhelmed, or in the case of Ellen's family, try to protect their upset child by avoiding the topic.

Ellen (16)

Ellen and her family came to therapy because she had fondled her younger brother. She had done it on several occasions, and when her brother told their mother, Ellen initially denied it. A counselor ended their first counseling experience because Ellen couldn't talk about it. The family ended their second attempt at therapy because Ellen was just seen individually and the parents were given no direction. I was their third therapist, this time court-ordered.

Ellen was smart, and she knew the language of feelings and behaviors, but presented it all in a monotone or heady way. She smiled only once at that first session when I asked her about her best friend. It showed an innocence deeper than her painted eyes and purple-streaked, black hair.

Her parents made it clear that they preferred to be involved in the sessions with her, but they did not want their four other children to attend. I explained that I could only work with them if I could see Ellen individually twice per month and the entire family for sessions twice per month. When I said the sessions would alternate between an individual session one week and a family session the next week, Ellen abruptly agreed. Her parents were hesitant, but also agreed by saying, "We'll take it one month at a time."

Because Ellen was fairly verbal, her individual sessions went smoothly. She told me about her friends, her boyfriend, and eventually even her behavior with her brother. She explained life on their hobby farm and the hassles of feeding their few animals before going to school. "I hate getting up so early when I already have to get up early for school." She talked of laughing with her sister and three brothers while watching their horses and many dogs mating. It was from those funny scenes that she thought she got the idea to see how her brother's penis worked. She didn't feel good about doing it, but "he laughed sometimes when I did it, so at first I did-n't think it was that bad."

The flow of her individual sessions was not present in their family sessions. In particular, on one occasion I explained that later we would begin doing the family sexuality education series. Ellen's mom flared-up by saying, "Now that's only going to happen with me, my husband, and Ellen in the session. The younger ones have had enough of this sex stuff, and all they do is cry when the topic is brought up."

Exploring her concerns further, I discovered how discussions or questions in their family regarding sex and Ellen's behavior usually became heated, and family members would walk off to their rooms in anger. Ellen's mother was most concerned about one of the boys who was not involved in the negative sexual behavior. "He always hears what's going on in bits and pieces, and because we're all mad, he gets upset and hides in his room." Due to the mother's concern, I did not schedule the sexuality series until another month had passed. Later, with fear in her face and hesitation in her voice, Ellen's mother reluctantly agreed to the family sex education series.

Ellen's mother was right. Immediately after the sex education series began, the younger kids' heads went down and the second to the youngest's eyes filled with tears. I calmly stated that anyone who needed a break could take one in my waiting room, and no one had to talk if they felt uncomfortable. I continued asking Mom and Dad questions regarding when and how they had learned about sex, who they currently talked about it with, and what they wanted to pass on to their kids. After briefly asking the kids similar questions, I went on to talking about male and female bodies, using charts and pictures. My language was filled with positive words, and my voice was open to anything shared by any family member. Within ten minutes, the three youngest children were on their knees directly in front of me. They were looking closer at the charts and pictures and asking more questions than anyone had predicted or imagined. When I looked up at Ellen's mother, she was nodding her head, with tears in her eyes. As she later said, "I couldn't believe how much they wanted to know, and how comfortable they were talking about the whole sex topic in a different way."

Ellen's family, especially her younger siblings, successfully completed the family sexuality series. They were able to refer to and ask about sex in future family sessions with confidence and comfort. Ellen's apology session was very sincere and personal, with all her siblings helping her by listening and supporting both her and her brother, whom she had inappropriately touched.

Although the sexuality aspect of individual and family therapy sessions went well, there were certainly other issues that needed acknowledgement and change. For example, her father's attitudes about girls and women being subservient to boys and men; a past uncomfortable sexual encounter for her and her friend; and the need and desire on both her and her mother's part for closer mother/daughter communication. These were all areas that with discussion and change improved Ellen's situation, but all with

positive sexuality being one of the significant keys to the family learning how to help themselves through positive dialogue.

Ellen's situation is not unusual for the families I see in therapy. On the contrary, the majority of the families I have seen in therapy have communication discomforts. Sexuality is one of those areas, and I have discovered that open, positive discussion leads to new-found comfort in other areas. Families are nervous and hesitant initially; however, within two or three sessions these families experience a closer way of relating and communicating that was not previously present. Not all of these families experience one of their children choosing inappropriate sexual behavior, but many of them disclose the confusion, fear, and worry about sex in their kids' lives and the problem of not knowing how to address the topic. However, the topic can, and needs to be, periodically addressed by parents. For example, with young children, while tucking them into bed at night, a parent could say, "You know, when I was your age I always saw this commercial where a girl was walking down a street and all the boys were turning their heads to look at her and then bumping into something. I never understood why the boys were bumping into things just to look at her. When I got older I realized it was because she had changed the color of her hair so all the boys would notice her. And I thought, 'Well, that's dumb. Why don't the boys just notice her because she's a nice person, not just because of her hair color?' So how about you? Are there any commercials that you ever wonder about or don't know what they mean?"

With a young teenager, while driving in the car a parent could say, "I like some of the songs on your radio station, but sometimes this deejay sounds too silly because he's always trying to joke about sex. Do you notice that too, or are you used to it?"

Talking about sexuality in a more personal way not only creates closeness on other personal topics, it also helps kids expand their perspective. My belief is that many children and teenagers are unconsciously led into inappropriate sexual behavior because they are witness to our narrowly focused media and have nothing healthy to contrast it to. To include practice on personal topics such as sexuality enables families to become stronger and more open than the media. This developed strength in families creates a solid basis of trust which helps children and teenagers thrive beyond, and become wiser than the media's glitzy presentations.

In Ellen's family, their openness and comfort with each other began and was made complete by the sexuality discussions in healthy ways. It paved the way for other personal topics which would likely not have been addressed without taking on the ever-present subtle and blatant sexual messages the children and teenagers were being exposed to. Families need to talk about all personal topics, including sexuality, in order to have children and teenagers develop confidence prior to going out into and surviving in the world. Other personal topics include support of feelings expression in respectful ways, listening and not reacting too quickly to your children's and teenagers' dreams and different opinions, verbal and physical expressions of love and affection, and always hearing what your kids have to say respectfully, even when it's surprising.

Age-Appropriate Preparing

In preparing children and teenagers for life in America, parents need to address personal topics in age appropriate ways. In the area of sexuality, age-appropriate actions for toddlers would be experiencing family baths, openly changing clothes, and proper naming of all body parts, including their penis or vagina. For preschoolers, age—appropriate sexuality would be a continuation of what they experienced and learned as a toddler, with the added availability of respectful picture books or magazines depicting happy, unclothed people of all ages, body types and race. For kindergarteners answering the question, "Where do babies come from?" parents should answer, "They come from inside Mommy's body, in her uterus, which is by her tummy."

For children first through third grade, age-appropriate sexuality would include what they've already experienced and learned, as well as beginning picture books and general talk about how babies are created. The viewing

of picture books and conversations should be short and easy, but always include proper naming of body parts, how they work together, and saying how two people's love makes intimate touch appropriate. For children fourth through sixth grade, age-appropriate sexuality includes ongoing, casual family changing of clothes and use of the bathroom, healthy picture books and magazines of happy, unclothed people of all ages, body types and races, as well as ongoing talks which include more physical and emotional detail of lovemaking, relationship commitment, and babies.

For young people seventh through ninth grade, age-appropriate sexuality includes what they have experienced at younger ages, with the added discussion of relationship—building through listening and compromising, and learning to identify healthy and unhealthy sexuality aspects of the media, movies, and immature adults focusing on and using sex as a weapon, manipulation, or for money.

For teenagers tenth through twelfth grade, age-appropriate sexuality includes previous experiences and discussions, if they are open to it, listening to and supporting their friendships and boyfriend/girlfriend decisions, and encouraging and practicing their openness on sexual matters with their significant others. As they become seniors in high school and approach 17 and 18 years old, the parental connection needs to be one of listening, support, and broad guidelines, rather than day-to-day parenting on their habits and developing lifestyle.

Age-Appropriate Talk and Actions

Toddlers	Using proper names for all body parts, with acceptance for self-exploration. Family baths and openly changing of clothes.
Preschool and Kindergartners	Respectful picture books depicting happy, unclothed people of all ages, body types, and race. Answering their question of where babies come from: from inside Mommy's body/uterus.
1st to 3rd Grade	Viewing picture books on how babies are created and born. How intimate touch and special hugs are appropriate and good if two people love each other. That the penis and vagina coming together in a special hug can start a baby growing in the uterus.
4th to 6th Grade	Highlighting the emotional, caring aspects of lovemaking, special hugs and relationship commitment. Openly judging movies or TV as real caring or shallow.
7th to 9th Grade	Picture books depicting the intimate, physical aspects of lovemaking in caring ways, relationship building through listening and compromising, and identifying people who use sex as a weapon, manipulation, or money.
10th to 11th Grade	Supporting boyfriend/girlfriend choices, their newly forming opinions on sexuality, and giving more independence as they become responsible.
12th Grade and turning 18	Supporting and accepting their decisions even when not informed of all their choices. Giving broad guidelines rather than parenting day to day on their habits and developing lifestyles.

Children and teenagers who are raised with these age-appropriate sexual talks and experiences are not only ahead of most of their peers, but are also wiser than the media. By preparing and parenting beyond, parents have the courage to say and teach more completely than what the media is constantly alluding to. It includes not only talking about sexuality and what the media is referring to, but also showing respectful and caring picture books and magazines of human bodies and intimate affection.

Although these ideas may sound radical or extreme, they are certainly far more respectful than what the media is doing in sexual ways to our children and teenagers. Parenting beyond does involve outside-of-thenorm type of parenting. The ideas and suggestions are meant to develop a maturity in children and teenagers that will take them beyond what they see in the media and around them. It can be done step-by-step and at a pace that's comfortable, but it must be done if parents want caring, respectful, and knowledgeable young people. It is exactly these traits that will carry them beyond the tricky, manipulative, negative sexual messages that the media throws at them daily.

Advertisers, movie, and television producers are not the ones who care about the completely safe growth of our children; they're focused on surviving and making money, and they need our young people to do it. While the media people are busy plotting ways to get our young people's attention and money, we had better be doing some excellent parenting. Putting our heads in the sand and hoping or waiting for new laws to curtail these negative sexual messages from the media is sacrificing our young people. In the meantime, while a parent is waiting, their kids are being bombarded by the negative effects of the media. Our task is to take steps now to ensure our young people's emotional and sexual health before it's too late.

Seeing is Believing

If children and teenagers actually see their parents occasionally engaging in caring conversations about sexuality and respecting their own bodies in open ways, then they really begin to believe that sexuality is special and very different from just seeing an unclothed body. The attitude that unclothed bodies and nudity means a sexual turn on is inappropriate and wrong. It is a by-product of the media and of a society where sexuality is not frequently talked about in caring ways. However, this message has been imprinted in our kids' minds, due to our society's current influence and upbringing norms. It doesn't belong there, because it develops kids that are selfish, shallow-minded, and who hold a narrow viewpoint of human bodies and relationships.

If adults don't take physical action in the form of new behavior toward open talks and casual family openness to unclothed bodies, children, and especially teenagers, will remain shallow and become perfectly-groomed consumers of the media. They will spend much of their time and energy trying to emulate a few popular models, movie stars, or boorish athletes whose pictures grace the covers of most magazines. The answer is not in parents trying to lecture their kids about the inappropriateness or negative ways of the media. The real answer is deeper and more encompassing than just words.

Gestures

The only way parents can prioritize sexuality in a positive way is through gestures—open talking gestures and respectful, behavioral gestures. Talking gestures are actually initiating dialogue on sexuality, and behavioral gestures are actually doing something different; i.e. becoming more casually open when changing clothes or using the bathroom with young children, or purposefully not attending a movie with a teenager because of its display of sexual touch outside of a committed relationship.

Behavioral Gestures

Any action or behavior a parent engages in that promotes a healthy and respectful outlook toward sexuality is a positive behavioral gesture. For parents of toddlers, gestures include taking baths together, changing clothes with doors open, and allowing them to touch their own genitals in exploration. For parents of young children, gestures include a continuation of changing clothes with doors open, skinny-dipping on a family camping trip, and having respectful picture books available of all types of unclothed human bodies. For parents of middle-aged children, gestures include a continuation of having respectful picture books of all types of unclothed human bodies available, some caring pictures of intimate touch between human beings available, and actually not watching a certain television show or listening to a radio disk jockey because they are sexually disrespectful. For parents of teenagers, gestures include a continuation of respectful picture books being available, inviting them to attend a march against pornography in the community, or a letter to the newspaper editor stating an opinion about healthy or unhealthy sexuality, and allowing them to have their own opinions about sexuality and intimacy.

It is important to note that there is a considerable difference between body comfort among family members and sexual flirting within a family. Parents and kids who walk from the bathroom in their underwear or a towel and talk normally or merely go about their business are being respectful and natural. Parents who allow or make provocative comments or innuendoes when a family member is in their underwear or a towel are sexualizing the individual, and therefore acting disrespectfully and shallow. Too often parents try to be "friends" with their kids, and within that atmosphere act inappropriately by making sexualized comments and laughing. However, for a parent to engage in such banter or promiscuousness demeans and sexualizes their own children or teenagers. It is the good parent who can appropriately step back and allow their kids and their friends to talk frivolously without interfering. These parents also create a family atmosphere where their kids do not make sexual jokes. This sort of age-appropriate boundaries that a parent is establishing by their own actions and what they expect of their kids, not only teaches respect, but also individual privacy on certain personal matters.

Behavioral gestures do not need to be done frequently. If they are acted on periodically, that is often enough to set the tone for a broader and more respectful picture of sexuality. Gestures help kids see beyond the media and give them a deeper respect and understanding of themselves and relationships in general. Seeing how the real world works and what one can do to respectfully express their beliefs and possibly change a negative standard provides satisfaction and personal confidence.

Talking Gestures

In a practical sense, parents don't really have a choice in this matter. They have to talk about sexuality or their children and teenagers won't talk about it. Why would they? If their parents are so uncomfortable addressing sexuality and talking about it openly in their lives, it is highly unlikely that their own kids would comfortably bring it up or talk much about it with them. A teenager is usually more comfortable talking with their friends, and because it is not their job to help their parents become comfortable, they will continue dealing with the topic with friends instead of their parents. However, if a parent can bring up sexuality topics from a young age with their kids in the form of openness, fun, exploring curiosities together, and acceptance of their kids opinions, then they have their attention. Maintaining kids' attention is easier than trying to gain attention for the first time, and it gives kids a broader and more complete knowledge base than if they were only talking with their friends.

Positive talking gestures can start out simple. For example, after watching a movie with young children, a parent could briefly say, "I like the way Mark treated his girlfriend. I could feel close to him. But I didn't like the way John always interrupted his girlfriend. I don't think I could trust him." Sometimes kids will pick up on this, and other times they won't. Either way, accept it. Don't push it. Inviting them by commenting is sometimes enough, because at least the topic is being verbalized openly.

As parents of teens, the statements have to be much more revealing. For example; "I had a boyfriend once like Mark and it made it easy to say 'no' to sex. But when I had some like John, they just never got it, so we broke up after about a month."

If teenagers ask questions about what you said or bring up comments themselves, make sure you don't turn it into a lesson for them. Ask them questions, too. Hear what they say and how they came to believe what they said. Wait for them to ask a question and then lightly answer what you know to be true. If you don't really know, ask openly "Where could we find out?" Teens will be more likely to talk and ask more questions as time goes on if they feel you're not judging them or that you're not going off on a lecture about life and love.

A typical conversation may go something like this:

"Mom, did you ever have sex when you were a teenager?"

After the shock wears off and you regain your composure, answer honestly.

"Whew, that's a personal question and really catches me off guard, but I'm glad you feel comfortable enough to ask. As you know, our conversation is just between us, in the family, right?"

"Yeah, yeah, I know that."

"Okay, good. Well, in a way, yes, I did have some sex and in a way I didn't. When I was a teenager, sex—meaning intercourse—was very rare. But I did have some boyfriends in high school that I felt close enough to that once in awhile, while we were kissing, we would touch each other intimately. I know there were a few times with one of my favorite boyfriends where he touched my breasts and I touched his butt."

"Yeah, but did you ever really have sex?"

"Well, no, not until I was in college and I had been going with him for almost a year. We talked ahead of time and I got on the pill."

"Were you scared?"

"Just a little, but at the time I loved him and we trusted each other. Why do you ask? Are you dealing with sex now?"

"No, but everybody's talking about it. I just wondered what it will be like when I get to high school this fall."

"Oh, what have you heard?"

"Well, that some of the guys kind of expect sex if you're going together."

"What do you think about that?"

"I don't know, but if I like him I can see getting into some of it."

"Do you think you'd be able to talk about it with him?"

"I don't know. Most people don't really talk about it. Don't you just kind of know?"

"I don't think so. That's more of a guessing game. It may work out, but often times it doesn't. I always felt that if I could talk about it with him, I could trust him. If it was the kind of talk he was open to, that was a good sign. If he wasn't, I held back."

"Yeah, but it sounds so dumb to talk about it. What am I going to say, 'Well, do you want to talk about sex?' Nobody does that, Mom."

"I know, and I'm not saying it's easy. But something like, 'I like the way we touch, but did it seem kind of heavy to you the other night? Do you think we should slow down a little?' Plus, you can see where he goes with it. What he says will tell you a lot about being comfortable and trusting with him."

"Oh, Mom, I don't know."

"Well, that's okay. It's just good to think out loud and talk about these things with someone you trust. Let's talk again some other time, because I know it's important to go slow with intimacy."

"Why do you have to go slow?"

"Because real intimacy only happens if a deep trust is there, along with caring about each other."

"Mmmm."

Conversations like this are really an opening to later discussions about intimate sexual touch and sexual intercourse. The parent in this conversation plays a good parent, in that she is not judgmental about her daughter or her peer group. She keeps the focus on what her daughter thinks and she expresses her own beliefs and hopes without pressure. This type of parenting keeps the lines of communication open and gives the teenager something to think about. She knows there are other ways to do things besides the peer group, and now she has the time and openness in communication with her mother to think about what she wants.

Some people criticize this kind of parenting. However, I call it an "instilling maturity" type of parenting. Strictness and opinions will get teenagers to close up and act out impulsively because tough issues are really never talked through, and talking through issues takes several conversations. Openness in sharing one's own beliefs gets teenagers to think, to listen, and to talk about it more than once.

Another reason I call it 'instilling maturity' parenting is that it's based on the belief that teenagers are developing their true personalities. It is not based on the belief that a parent has to develop and teach their teen how to be! It gives time for self-exploring thought on the part of the teenager, rather than the parent imposing a set of beliefs they feel should be upheld by their teen. It also invites growth and self-discovery, rather than stifling their thoughts by forcing rote memorizations on them. That approach closes off a teen's deeper thoughts and makes non-thinking about roles a habit. More open parenting usually invites dialogue, discussion, and deep learning on the part of teenagers.

Granted, there are times when a teen chooses an inappropriate behavior and needs to be given a consequence; however, a parent makes a grave mistake if during the giving of the consequence they allow their anger to take over. This happens when a parent goes on and on instead of focusing on just the behavior and the consequence. They start to call into question their teen's whole belief system by going on as if she didn't have such a different attitude about things, this would've never happened. Or if she would just settle down and stop acting like she knows everything. At this point it has become an attack on a teen's personality type and beliefs, not just on the isolated behavior and the appropriate consequence. If a parent mixes these two concepts, a great hindrance is put onto the openness in their relationship and on their teen's moral and character development. When a behavior is inappropriate, a parent must keep the focus on that and no more. When a discussion of beliefs takes place, keep the focus on that and not their behavior. The results of mixing these two important areas is that a parent loses the opportunity for close communication with their teen, and the chance for an important life lesson is lost. Whether it's a discussion about their behavior, angry feelings, or sex, a teenager will only listen deeply if they believe and see, through their parent's actions, that the parent still loves, likes, and respects them.

In the area of sexuality, this type of seasoned parenting is paramount. A teen needs to walk away from a discussion with their parent knowing two things: one, that they were really listened to and respected for what they said; and two, that they really know how their folks feel and why. The "why" is learned by hearing their parents' experiences and mistakes. The feelings are learned by the parent neutrally expressing their own viewpoints and not lecturing about what their teen should or should not do.

A conversation with a teenage boy may go something like this.

"So, son, how's it going at your new school?"

"Ahh, it's okay, I guess."

"Yeah, well tell me, what's it like for someone to be in 9th grade at your school?"

"I don't know. Just normal, I guess."

"Is it a lot different from 8th grade?"

"Yeah."

"Mmm. What's one of the biggest differences?"

"Well, there's more time to talk with your friends between classes."

"Oh."

"And it's a lot more cliquey."

"What do you mean?"

"Certain groups of kids hang out together and they don't mix around too much."

"Are you in a group you like?"

"Yeah, because I'm with a lot of the kids I was with last year."

"Do you get along with the other groups?"

"Some of them."

"Tell me more. I like listening to you."

"Dad…"

"Come on, you've got such interesting things going on in your life. I like to listen."

"Well, some of the groups are cool, but some are mean."

"Really."

"Yeah, like this one group of guys is always trying to be tough. We just avoid them. And this other group is always after the hot girls and they think they're so cool."

"Are you and your friends after the hot girls?"

"Not like those guys. They're mean. If a girl doesn't talk or hang out with them, they kind of harass her."

"What do you guys do?"

"We're just friendly and if they are too, we talk. If not, we both go our own ways."

"Sounds good. What about the girls that are harassed? Is it in kind of a sexual way?"

"Well, they don't always pick on the girls; sometimes you just hear them bragging about what they wish they'd done. At least that's what we think, because there's no way those guys go that far with so many different girls."

"Oh, you mean bragging about what they did with a girl the night before?"

"Yeah, and sometimes you just know they weren't even together."

"Do you and your friends ever get into that kind of bragging or joking around?"

"No. We might joke, but we don't brag about anything. Why, Dad? Did you when you were in high school?"

"Not really, but sometimes I found it hard not to get caught up in the talk."

"What do you mean?"

"When I was in school it was really cool for guys to brag about what they did sexually with a girl. And although I was one of the quieter guys when it came to bragging, I would laugh with them, and maybe make a

comment about doing more than I did."

"Sometimes we might make a comment like that, but not much."

"Oh...how is it for you when you're talking to your friends about girls and sex?"

"Well, I don't really say much, but I listen to the other guys. And then I wonder what I'll do with my girlfriend, someday, when I have one."

"And do you wonder if you'll talk about it later with the guys?"

"Yeah, kind of, maybe."

"Good luck on that one, son, because it's tough. I admit I wished I had-n't said something to the guys about one of my girlfriends."

"Why? Did it get back to her?"

"No, but I just felt bad about it, like I'd betrayed her trust. I always felt better being open with her and not talking behind her back."

"You mean talk to her about sexual stuff?"

"Yeah. Do you think you could talk to your girlfriend about sexual stuff?"

"I don't know. In a way I'd like to, but I wouldn't want to make her uncomfortable."

"That's a good point, son, and all I can say is it was hard at first, but I'm glad I did. I think she was glad, too, because after that talk we were both more comfortable with the whole topic."

"Really."

"Yes. As a matter of fact, we should ask your mom and sister about this because they could give us the girl's viewpoint."

As you can see, the father is sharing some of his own history, is inquisitive of his son's current situation, and he keeps it open by including Mom and sister in further discussion. Open. Non-judgmental. Continued conversation.

Many teens don't start out by asking a parent the question, so other possible lead-in questions by a parent might go something like this:

"So, Sara, what's the best thing about boys at your school?"

The question keeps the initial focus not so squarely on the teen and can be brought to different topic areas such as "What's it like switching classes?" "What's it like at lunch?" "What's it like when the boys are being mean?"

"John, what did you think of that movie we saw last night?"

Again, a general lead in just to start the conversation, then a parent can bring it deeper. "What did you think of the way he acted around his girlfriend?" "What did you think of the way she got back at him when she was mad?" "Who was your favorite character or least favorite?"

"Sara, when I was in school the guy always asked the girl on a date and paid for everything. What's it like now?"

"John, when I was younger, all my girlfriends passed messages to each other and to a guy so he would ask a girl out. What's it like now?"

"How do you handle it now when someone you don't really like romantically asks you out?"

Always be ready to answer the questions yourself, and always be calmly ready to listen. Teenagers will usually talk and open up if they feel like you really care to know and you're not going to judge them. There is a difference between judging a teenager and setting limits with consequences.

For example, a judgmental parent will say, "I don't ever want to hear of you being sexual with a boy/girl." An open parent will say, "What do you think would be the fairest way to handle it if we found out you were sexual with your girlfriend/boyfriend?"

The assumption in the open parent is that something will happen, and it will be discussed; however, it's open to negotiation. In the judgmental parent, the teenager is already getting some of the parent's anger before they have done anything. Fear may stop certain behaviors in the moment, but it also erodes self-confidence, and therefore it is more destructive to their maturity in the long run.

Another example would be a judgmental parent saying, "If I ever catch you using drugs, don't even call for a ride, because you're going right to detox." An open parent might say, "Now, you know how I feel about drugs. Don't use them. But if ever you do by mistake, or experimentally, or whatever, call me. I'll come and get you and make sure you're safe, and then we can talk about it the next day." The following day it can be handled calmly and strictly.

Parenting teens around sexual issues is very difficult because you want to instill independence and maturity, while at the same time helping them to understand the importance of holding off, or at least going slow. Teens want to experiment, learn things for themselves, and some times just rebel. A parent has a tough job trying to strike a balance. With the parents I see in my practice, I recommend the accessible or open approach. This approach involves a conversation that may go something like this: "Now, I know this is a big night with Prom and all, so I want you to really enjoy yourself and have fun. I also want you to be careful. I hope you choose to stay away from any drug use and I hope you choose not to be sexually active. I know you may feel differently because of what you have said in our talks, but consider what I've said, too. You'll feel better if you wait, and you might as well have fun and feel good the next day, instead of worried or depressed because you went too far. You know about calling us if you should use drugs, and you know about condoms and safe sex if you decide differently than what we believe. I hope you choose comfort and safety for yourself, but if you can't or don't, call us. Your mom and I will be thinking about you and know you'll have a fun time. We love you and would do anything to help you."

This type of message to a teen could even be put in a letter with a gift of money for the evening or something special. Some parents have felt that to say the message the way I recommend gives subtle permission to try sex; just do it safely. In my practice, I haven't found that to be true. What I have found is that many teenagers might "try out" some form of sexual intimacy; however, because they are accustomed to talking about sex they generally go slower and use precautions. Also, the teens with open parents will often talk about it, and therefore seem to put sex in perspective quicker

than the teens that don't talk about it. Sex is not the biggest part of their relationships. With the non-talking parents, teens don't talk about it later, and sex seems to be central to all their relationships, and is therefore a constant focus.

As parents, much is gained in terms of substantive thinking by inviting and keeping teens talking about what they're doing. If they talk, they tend to learn and go slower than the crowd. If they don't or can't talk, they usually keep pushing the limits and continually attempt to learn on their own. Certainly a result of some of these talks may be cautioning them or discussing how trust is earned or diminished. However, the focus of parenting teens is not to completely prevent them from possible negative experiences or situations, but rather to help them grow through their mistakes calmly. Talk and self-awareness go a long way in helping teenagers become safe, good decision makers. Not talking keeps too much mystery in their world and so naturally, they will often explore impulsively.

Teenagers will not always be open to talking, and often your invitations to talk will be rebuffed. This is normal and should not be taken personally. They will talk sometimes, and that is extremely important when parenting teens. A parent needs to remember that the primary developmental task of the teenager is to slowly pull away from their family and begin creating their own identity. This should not be done all in their eighteenth year. It needs to be a process, beginning at approximately age 13 and building to their eighteenth year. Small steps at first, but parents must always give more independence as they grow, and when they make mistakes, the chance to try again.

Importance of Talking with Younger Children

The thought of teaching very young children about sexuality makes many parents extremely uncomfortable. They are concerned about taking away their child's innocence or believe they should wait until their young ones ask questions. Nothing could be further from the truth or what's best for children. What's best is that young children grow into knowledge and learning about sexuality from their parents. If children's learning and experience has a source other than their parents, they are at a disadvantage. To let such an important topic lie on the outskirts of conversation only gives the media more influence and maintains shallow-thinking kids. For parents to let sexuality talks come about naturally or when their kids ask questions is only a subtle form of avoidance, and avoidance when parenting creates lost or mistrusting children. They simply cannot learn or trust in healthy ways without primary parent involvement and guidance. From the point when children begin to remember (ages 3-5), sexual messages begin to accumulate in their minds. Whether they see their mom and dad kiss, hear sexual jokes, or watch television, they're taking in sexual messages. If it is from the media, most of them are negative and shallow. If they are from family and their dad and mom, most of it is unexplained and not talked about. This type of upbringing in sexuality, through the eyes of a child, is extremely limiting and confusing. Without early and frequent parental input, one can understand why children don't ask questions, try to avoid the topic like their parents, and come to view sex as an excitingly bad thing. Anything short of bringing up sexual topics and explaining concepts respectfully and briefly is a negative setup because it sends kids out into their world unprepared.

Some sexual messages do not deeply affect children; however, many are retained. If parents broach sexual topics lightly and briefly in normal conversations, children not only comfortably fit the topic into their life and conversations, but can also filter out and put in perspective what they are witnessing. Usually a sentence or two is enough for young children. Following are example questions and answers for young children:

"Where did Aunt Mary's baby come from?"

"Remember how her tummy was big? Well, that's where babies come from—inside their mommy's body. They start out tiny, and when they grow big enough they come out and are born."

"Daddy, how did the baby get inside Aunt Mary's tummy?"

"When a dad and mom love each other a lot, sometimes they hug and hold each other, and sometimes that can start a baby growing."

"Mommy, how do Aunt Mary and Uncle John know if a baby will start to grow when they're hugging?"

"Well, sometimes when they hug, it's a regular hug with their clothes on. Other times it's a special hug when they're alone, and it's from the special hugs that sometimes a baby will begin to grow."

"Daddy, why do Aunt Mary and Uncle John do hugs alone?"

"Because when a mom and mad really love each other a lot they feel happy and special to be alone sometimes and hug."

"Yeah, but how does that make a baby start to grow?"

"When a dad and mom have a special hug when they're alone they have their clothes off so they can be really close together, and that feels very loving."

"Mommy, do you and Daddy sometimes have special hugs like Aunt Mary and Uncle John?"

"Yes, honey, and that's how you came about and started to grow inside of me."

"Daddy, why do you have to take off your clothes so a baby starts to grow?"

"Because that kind of special hug you only have with the one person you love, and when your clothes are off and you hug that special person you're in love with your bodies come together and the man's penis and the woman's vagina also come together."

"Mommy, how does the special hug with no clothes on make a baby start to grow?"

"Because there's a special egg inside of the mom's body and a special sperm inside the dad's body, and when the vagina and penis come together the special sperm from the dad comes together with the special egg inside the mom, and whenever the mom's egg and the dad's sperm came together, that's when a baby will start to grow."

"What's a sperm?"

"A sperm is like a special seed inside the dad's body that can meet the mom's special egg when their vagina and penis come together in a special hug."

With some children, parents will have to bring up sexually related topics because many children do not. It's important to go slow, to invite rather than overwhelm young children with questions, and only bring up the topic periodically—once a week for just a few minutes. Following are examples of inviting conversation:

"Mary, do you ever wonder how babies are made?"

"Yes, but I know."

"Oh, how are they made?"

"Well, it just happens when a mom and dad get married."

"That's good, Mary. I also wanted to tell you that it happens when a mom and dad have special hugs."

"Like the special hugs you give me?"

"A little different. I give you mommy and daughter special hugs. A dad and mom have their own kind of special hug, too."

"Johnny, in that television show you saw with your friend's brother, did you think it was kind of funny the way that boy kept trying to kiss and hug that girl?"

"Yeah, I didn't look, Dad, because I don't like that."

"Oh, sure, that's okay, son. I was just going to tell you why boys and girls do that sometimes. Would you like to know?"

"Mmm, I don't care."

"Well, if you've ever wondered, it's because when a boy and a girl like each other, when they get older, it feels nice and happy when they hug or touch each other in those special ways, and it's really nice and happy the more they really like each other."

"Yeah, well, she didn't want to kiss him very much."

"That's right, Johnny, and that's why he should have stopped, because it only really counts or feels nice if both of the people like each other."

"Yeah, I know that."

"Well, good for you. It's always nice talking about neat things like this with you."

"Mary, what did you think when all the kids were laughing at Julie's dogs humping?"

"It was funny."

"Do you know why dogs do that?"

"No."

"Would you like to know?"

"Yeah."

"Well, they are like all animals, and to have puppies or babies, the girl dog and boy dog need to bring their penis and vagina together, and then a couple of months later puppies are born."

"Why do they have to do that?"

"Because there's a special egg inside a girl dog and a special sperm or seed inside a boy dog that have to come together, and it's the girl dog's vagina and the boy dog's penis that brings them together."

"Oh."

"It's kind of the same with people, only the mom and dad who love each other do it in a more gentle, loving way when they hug each other in a special way."

"That's funny."

"Yeah, sometimes it sounds funny, doesn't it? But when two people hug each other in that gentle, special way, it feels very nice and makes them happy."

There are many ways to be open with young children and slowly allow them to experience truthful and comfortable communication. It doesn't matter how little is talked about, as long as parents initiate it and maintain it.

This is a conversation a mother had with her 5-year-old boy during a family sex education session.

"Mommy, I saw a picture of a lady and she was flat."

"Oh, what do you mean, she was flat?"

"She was flat down here; she didn't have a penis."

"Oh, in her private spot?"

"Yeah, she didn't have a penis like me."

"Well, you know what?"

"What?"

"On a boy that part of the body is called a penis and on a girl that part of the body is called a vagina."

"Why?"

"I don't know. That's just the way God made boys and girls."

"Mom, do I still get to watch a video today?"

"Yes, you do, honey."

"Good, because I really like my new movie."

"I know you do."

The little boy looked at some pictures I had taken out of my bookcase and continued.

"I see her boobies, Mom."

"Yes, and do you know what I like to call that part of my body?"

"What?"

"Breasts."

"Can I poke them?"

"No, because only I touch my private spots and sometimes your dad when we have special hugs."

"How come he can and I can't?"

"Because you're not an adult yet and not in love and married. And that's why for you and all kids, only you can touch your own private parts."

"What do you call these again?"

"Breasts."

"Oh, yeah. Mom, can we color with these new crayons now?"

"Sure we can."

Her conversation flowed comfortably among body parts, videos, intimacy, and coloring. As long as she periodically addressed intimacy and private parts with her son, he would likely keep talking about sexuality with her. If not, she could gently remind him that talk about bodies, babies, and touch is so special that only families talk about it. Talk with friends and sex education teachers comes later. However, if she does not bring up the topic again or does not have ongoing attention for him, then his chances of talking about sex outside of his family also increases.

Ryan (4)

Ryan attended therapy with his family because his teenage brother had verbally and sexually harassed a girl at school. The parents were supportive and also willing to have the entire family attend the family sex education sessions. Ryan's brother, sisters, and parents all contributed to the discussions. Periodically, during the session, Ryan's father noticed Ryan looking at someone who was talking. He politely said, "You can just play with your cars on the floor while we talk." Ryan was happy to do so. Smiling, the father looked at me and said, "I'm sure he has no idea what we're talking about."

At the end of the session I asked each family member if they had any questions or something more they wanted to say. When I got to Ryan, he stuck up his middle finger and said, " My brother does this to me sometimes."

His brother and sisters did not react, but his father sat back with his mouth open. I answered Ryan by saying we would put that behavior in the unhealthy or disrespectful type of sex rather than a healthy, respectful category. As they left my office, Ryan's father could only shake his head.

Like Ryan, many young children pick up numerous negative sexual messages by the age of four. Unchecked or not talked about in respectful ways, these negative messages are retained by young children, and too often they form the basis for their impressions in future learning about sexuality. This repeated pattern of negative sexual messages is the first step in the formation of a knowledge base that is limited, narrow-minded, and incomplete. As kids grow up in America with this kind of narrow and inappropriate exposure, it is understandable why they act out, and why the media continues to hold power over them. Without knowing a different way, our kids become trapped and remain pawns of the media, which of course is shallow, one-sided, limited in what is presented, and extremely sexist. And it is this repeated pattern, beginning at a young age, that sets up our young children for inappropriate and an incomplete initial exposure to sexuality and leads to a skewed learning process throughout their growing years. For our kids, there is simply too much exaggerated exposure to negative sexual messages in our society to expect them to grow past it unscathed or unaffected. The only viable solution is to insure that young children's first impression for sexuality is in positive, caring, and respectful experiences through involved parental openness and input.

The pattern of expecting others to teach and talk to our kids about sexuality is what keeps our children and teenagers truly distant from us. Whenever kids learn something personal from someone other than their parents and it is not followed up on by parents, a larger chasm forms between their two lives. Some separateness is normal and appropriate; for example, developing close friendships as they grow through their teenage years. However, separateness on significant and important life topics such as sexuality, drugs, or decision-making is unhealthy and poor parenting.

Steve (12) and Jim (13)

One particular family I worked with attended therapy because their two boys were caught drawing sexual graffiti in the school bathrooms. Apparently, their graffiti had been occurring regularly in different school bathrooms and school personnel were relieved when they discovered who the boys were, and happy to refer them to counseling. In the first session, Steve and Jim were honest about what they did, and much to their parents' frustration could not explain why they did it. "It was just funny," Steve said.

"Yeah, it was just for fun," Jim added.

After several attempts by their parents to get them to say why they did it, I asked the parents about sexual openness in their home. Both parents were surprised, but they answered sincerely.

"We've always been available if the boys had questions," Mom said. "We believed that if they asked us about sex, they were ready to learn about sex," their Dad stated.

I asked if the boys had brought up or asked sex-education type questions. After looking at each other for several seconds, both Mom and Dad shrugged and said they couldn't remember. Their dad then said, "I do remember one time Mr. Foster was teasing me at church about Steve and Jim's questions to him about his cows." Their dad explained that the boys would often walk through their backyard field and visit Mr. Foster while he milked his cows. Apparently, Steve and Jim were asking questions about how calves could be born without any male cows on his farm. Mr. Foster found the boy's questions amusing and at church took the chance to rib their father about it.

When I asked the boy's father what he did after his encounter with Mr. Foster, he said in anger, "When we got home, I told Steve and Jim to stop asking other people so many questions. If they need to know something they can come to me instead of embarrassing me with Mr. Foster."

The boys nodded when I asked if they remembered Mr. Foster and their father's words. Before I could ask another question, their mom brought up a situation.

"Of course there was that other time when I found that book under Steve's mattress."

As Steve and Jim dropped their heads, I asked about the book.

"It was a book called *Everything You Always wanted to Know about Sex but were Afraid to Ask*." She said it was an old paperback, and when she found it she yelled at Steve for having such a book and asked him why didn't he come to her if he had any questions. The boys kept looking down and did not say anything. When I looked back at their mother and father, I knew they could not see the irony in their angry and demanding attitude. If parents really want their kids to open up and talk about personal topics, they must be open to not only how their kids seek answers, but where. In Steve and Jim's family, the parents needed to see their sons' questions to the farmer and finding the book as an opportunity for openness. An approach of inviting questions would have gone a long way in developing dialogue and openness from their sons. For example, "I ran into Mr. Foster at church and he said you guys ask some pretty good questions. I'd like to talk about those questions with you guys too," or "Say, I saw your book when I was changing sheets. Boy, the author really gives good answers to some personal questions. Would you mind if I read it also and then we could compare what we've learned?"

The premise behind this approach is that parents can use uncomfortable moments concerning their kids as opportunities for deeper dialogue rather than as a lecture on family rules for avoiding embarrassment. It may take time to calm down after these types of uncomfortable experiences with kids, but the ensuing positive approach not only increases their knowledge base in respectful ways, it also brings a new level of closeness.

Parents can practice in role playing if they are uncomfortable or don't know what words to use when talking about sexuality. For example, one parent plays the role of a child or teenager and the other parent plays the role of the parent. The parent in the child's role asks questions and the parent in the parent's role answers as if they were in an actual situation with their child. After a few minutes, end the role playing and give feedback to each other. Tell each other what sounded good, what made sense, and what needs improvement. Another role-play is the parent in the parent's role practices different ways to bring up or ask about sex to the parent in the child's role. Again, after a few minutes, give feedback on what were comfortable ways of being asked, what was easy to answer, and what needs changing. Parents can practice these types of role plays several times before actually talking with their children or teenagers.

Another aspect that is significant to highlight with children and teenagers is the importance of lasting friendships and how they got that way. Because the media do the opposite by showing quick snaps of intimacy, it is understandable that many kids automatically believe that happiness comes from buying new things and that relationships can always be fun and fast-paced. However, reality is that one can't always be having fast-paced fun, or that buying new things doesn't always get a lot of fun attention from people. Good, fun, happy relationships are earned slowly over time, and its this kind of relationships that carry humans through life. A parent can give examples of friends who aren't really close, but are more like acquaintances. Talk about how they got that way. The reason may be that there is really no internal connection or that they're not the type of person to compromise or work things out. Then give examples of close friendships. Highlight the things that made those relationships extra close. It may be a natural ability to get along, a similar sense of humor, and an ability to work out tensions or disagreements. A good relationship is one that can get through the ups and downs of life. After sharing some of your own experiences with close and not-so-close friends, ask your child or teenager about some of their types of friendships. This kind of personal openness on the part of the parent usually invites and encourages children and teenagers to do the same. Although this type of conversation should not become too heavy or self-focused on the part of the parent, often they can become personally revealing in safe ways for children and teenagers.

Talking Even When Teens Say They Know

By the time kids are teenagers, they have seen significant amounts of the media and they have most likely talked and laughed a lot about sex with their friends. When teens say, "Oh, I know all about that," or "Don't talk about sex, we had all that in school," it's easy for a parent to let it go. As a parent, when this occurs believe that they've had a fair amount of sexual information through their friendships, school, and the media, but don't believe it's all they need. The information and laughter shared between friends, although important, is often incomplete. The angle of the media's presentation of sexuality is extremely slanted and narrow. And the sex education received during health class happens once, maybe twice in all of their years at school.

To have more complete sexual information, especially with a caring, emotional perspective and an ongoing understanding, teenagers need several sources that they can rely on for information. One of these important sources is parents. If their folks don't talk, teenagers continue learning elsewhere. It is necessary to learn from friends and school, but without their parents it is incomplete and often lacks the well-rounded, emotional impact that an open parent can provide.

Breaking the Ice

It's best not to focus too heavily on the importance of, and the need for talking about sex. It's better to just talk. This way teenagers won't feel so "on the spot," or as if they're being examined. Instead of talking about talking about sex, parents should just start discussing sex. Here are a few examples of questions that can open conversations with teenagers:

Example 1:

Parent: "Boy, what did you think of that guy in the movie? He sure seemed pushy and he was constantly trying to touch her."

Teen: "Yeah, but it's just a movie."

Parent: "What would you do if it really happened, because I remember what I did once."

Teen: "What? It really happened to you?"

Parent: "Oh, yes. I was at a school dance and this guy I didn't like kept asking me to slow dance. Finally I went up to him with two of my friends and said 'back off'."

Teen: "Did he?"

Parent: "Yes. I did catch him looking at me on and off, but he didn't ask me to dance any more."

Teen: "Creepy."

Parent: "Yeah, it was. How about you?"

Teen: "No, not really, but if it did I would have one of my guy friends tell him to give it a rest."

Parent: "Oh, that's a good idea."

Example 2:

Parent: "What's it like at your school when a girl is being too flirty with all the guys?"

Teen: "What do you mean? That happens all the time."

Parent: "Well, what do you think of the girls that do it a lot?"

Teen: "They're stupid, and everyone can see what they're doing. And I think there's no way I'm going to be that obvious."

Parent: "Oh, would you be more subtle?"

Teen: "Yeah, because I mean, getting a guy's attention and goofing around is okay. You just don't want it to get carried away."

Parent: "I like the way you think about that."

Example 3:

Parent: "I have an interesting question for you. How long do you think a couple should go out with each other before they get into intimate sex?"

Teen: "Mom, come on. Why are you asking me this?"

Parent: "Well, I'm just wondering if it's different than when I was young, and I like to hear your opinions about personal things, too."

Teen: "I'm sure it's different than when you were in high school because that was so long ago."

Parent: "Yes, it was, but I still remember it like it was yesterday. (Laugh) So what's the norm today?"

Teen: "Well, I don't know; it's different for different people."

Parent: "Yeah, well what's the range?"

Teen: "I don't know. Some people are that way after 3 months, and others wait longer."

Parent: "Oh, where are you in that range?"

Teen: "Well, I'm nowhere right now, because I'm not going with anybody."

Parent: "If you were, though, and you really liked him (or her), what would you be comfortable with?"

Teen: "I don't know; I'm not even thinking about that right now."

Parent: "I know, and I didn't mean to make you feel uncomfortable. I just like to know what you think about things."

Teen: "Yeah, well can we talk about this some other time?"

Parent: "Sure, now let's go get something to eat."

Example 4:

Parent: "Say, I wanted to get your personal thoughts on something."

Teen: "Oh yeah, what's that?"

Parent: "I know you and your friend have been going out together for a couple of months now and your friend seems really nice, so I was wondering if you've made any decision about sex yet?"

Teen: "Come on, we don't have to have this talk. I'm almost 17 and I know how to take care of myself."

Parent: "I know you do, and I'd like to talk about one of the ways you take care of yourself."

Teen: "Yeah, but I don't really need to know anything else."

Parent: "That may be true, but you know me, and this is one of the ways I still care about you, so what do you think? What have you decided about having or not having sex?"

Teen: "Well, I don't want to say what me and my friend do."

Parent: "Okay, that's fair. How about in a more general way then? Do you think intimate sex will be a part of your relationship if you're going with someone you really care about?"

Teen: "Well, yeah, if we really care about each other."

Parent: "Is it something you'll talk about, or will it kind of just happen?"

Teen: "I don't know, because it hasn't happened yet. I hope we would talk about it first."

Parent: "Yes, that's a good point, because if you're close enough to be that way, and if it's real, you should be able to talk about it first."

Teen: "Yeah, I know."

Parent: "One other thing I want to tell you."

Teen: "What?"

Parent: "I like your maturity about this topic, and even though we may feel differently about this, I hope you can hold off doing intimate touching until you're a bit older."

Teen: "Why?"

Parent: "Because when you do decide to have that kind of intimacy with someone you care about, it's nice, but it does add some emotional heaviness to your life."

Teen: "What, what do you mean?"

Parent: "Well, it's kind of a different example, but it's almost like getting your driver's license too soon. It's fun to drive on your own, but when you're not quite ready it adds more stress to your life. You think and worry about it because you're just not ready for that kind of responsibility. So with intimate touch it's similar. If you kind of get into it before you're really ready, or if you don't wait until you're a bit older, it adds a new dimension to life that can feel like a heaviness if you're not really ready for it."

Teen: "Yeah, but how do you know until you experience it?"

Parent: "Well, you kind of just feel or have an intuition about it. My feeling is at your age it's better to wait, and even though you are mature, it's okay to hold off for a while."

Teen: "Mmm."

Parent: "Now, if you do decide to become intimate, we will help you get birth control pills or whatever you need, because we'll always support you, but if you can, try to hold off, and I believe it will make a nice difference in the long run."

Teen: "Well, I'll think about it."

Parent: "Sounds good."

In these examples the parent keeps trying to dialogue, remains respectful, and keeps the conversation going. It is important to not let your teen's attitude or short remarks deter your efforts. You're doing it because you care, so don't let your teenager's mood change your mood. Keep trying. Keep caring. And always remain respectful.

When parenting around sexuality, it's important to remember three things:

One, we as parents and adults can no longer sit silently and wait for our children or teenagers to ask about sex. We need to speak up and break — the ice or they will learn very differently than we intend.

Two, in addition to talking, we have to act. Whether it's celebrating our teenagers becoming young men and young women, practicing casual family changing of clothes and bathroom use, or not attending a certain movie because it is disrespectful toward girls, we must go beyond our society's unhealthy presentation of sex and the human body. Three, we as parents must be open to learning from our children and teenagers. They see the world from different eyes and will often interpret things in a unique way. We need to listen and support their differences from us because it is not our job to tell them how to be. Rather, it is our responsibility and obligation to help our children and teenagers truly be themselves. This concept can be challenging, but it is the only attitude that can truly raise caring, knowledgeable, and respectfully strong kids. Anything less than openness, frequent dialogue, and respecting their different opinions shortchanges kids in our extremely busy society. The practice of open talks and respectful actions surrounding sexuality is one of the most significant ways to impart maturity and personal success onto our children and teenagers. It leaves them a strong legacy, unsurpassed by the fickle swayings of the media.

B.) The Action

Concrete Options for Parents and Communities

Taking concrete actions is the only viable and responsible option that America's parents have at this time. It is no longer acceptable, nor beneficial, to merely limit or keep kids away from inappropriate presentations of sex. If children experience limited exposure to sexuality or nothing at all, they remain empty, curious and naïve. This is a significant hindrance to their mental and emotional growth. Emotionally immature and naive kids are vulnerable kids.

They are vulnerable to the inappropriate messages and sway of sexual magazines and advertisements that use bodies to stimulate and provoke and television shows or radio disc jockeys who regularly use sexual innuendoes. These subtle messages begin to affect our kids negatively, because although they may be minor at the moment, they are continually occurring and become more frequent as children become teenagers. Although dealing with sex in open, caring, and respectful ways does counteract the negative focus of sexuality in our society, it is also the only way it should be taught naturally from the beginning. It ensures and teaches true respect for the opposite sex and their own bodies, as well as the strong development and well-roundedness of their whole personality.

Sex is only a natural act in two ways: one, the urge to be sexual; and two, the actual act itself. Everything else is learned. That includes the attitudes toward the opposite sex, dating norms, sex as just one part of intimacy, affection, touch, foreplay, using or giving in romantic relationships, approaching others with caring interest or a hidden agenda, what's okay to say and do and what's not okay, and relationship commitment. For parents to slowly open up and respectfully talk and act in caring ways about these sexuality topics encourages, enables, and ensures well-adjusted kids because they are learning within a trusted relationship.

Given the amount of negative and inappropriate exposure our kids are subject to in their daily lives, it becomes clear how important and significant taking concrete options in parenting can be. Prior to developing new and positive communication and concrete options when parenting kids, it's important to recognize and discontinue old habits. These may include some of the following:

A.) Letting kids watch MTV, sexualized sitcoms, and soap operas several hours each day. This creates "dead-pan eyes" and "emotional numbing," which can put flatness and low energy in their own lives. A good rule of thumb is one to two hours during the week and two to four hours on the weekend.

B.) Waiting for kids to bring up sexual questions for dialogue forms thick barriers in communication. Not explaining why sexual jokes or innuendoes are disrespectful and embarrassing forms further barriers. Also, becoming frustrated, angry, or noticeably uneasy when kids ask unusual questions adds to these barriers. Generally, any secretive or uncomfortable silence surrounding sex and sexuality maintains distance between parents and kids.

C.) Parents who are just trying to be funny or broach the relationship topic by teasing about girlfriends or boyfriends are actually hindering self-confidence, putting into question and doubt the need to belong in their peer group, and often hurting feelings. When this occurs, kids commonly close up their personal lives from their parents, and trust in communication is eroded. Boyfriends and girlfriends are an integral part of their lives, and within age-appropriate behavior must be treated in supportive ways.

D.) Making fun of, or laughing at people in sexual ways produces a cynicism that is not easily changed. This includes putting down boys who may cry or show tears with their emotions and laughing at or teasing girls who play contact sports. This type of indirect insulting by parents usually impedes trust, respect, and an equitable attitude toward the opposite sex.

E.) Parents make a mistake if they stop being affectionate with their children as they become teenagers. When this happens, many teenagers interpret it as being different because now they're physically and sexually maturing. As they grow, teenagers get the subtle message—by their parents' lack of affection—that touch should now take place only between boyfriends and girlfriends, and sometimes more dangerously, that touch is just for sex.

F.) Having pornographic magazines or sexual joke books in the home does immense damage to a daughter's self-esteem and hinders their developing independence. These kinds of materials focus too much importance on using women for men's entertainment or desires, and eventually sons begin to think they are better than girls.

G.) When parents say mean things or make fun of people who lead a different sexual lifestyle, animosity and intolerance are produced. Teenagers and children will either silently disagree and ignore their parents or follow in their parents' footsteps of ignorance. Both options have negative effects on kids. These destructive and unfortunately common habits must be uncovered and changed prior to any parent hoping to establish trust and mutual respect with their offspring. It is far more engaging and strengthening to approach kids in a positive, straightforward way.

Seven Ways to Raise Sexually Healthy Children and Teenagers.

1.) Openness from a young age.

Have healthy picture books openly placed around your home, from a child's young age, showing non-sexual nudity, smiles, and happiness. Bathe with your younger children and allow older children and teenagers to see you change clothes or get out of the shower. Give comfortable permission to skinny dip when on family camping trips, and consider sun-tanning and swimming at a clothes optional beach. This step is important, because it begins children's understanding of sexuality in a positive way. They see and learn about their bodies, other bodies, and opposite-sex bodies all before they learn about sex and procreation. This is an integral aspect of healthy sexuality—that there is a difference between unclothed bodies and sex. The two can and do exist independently of each other, and respect begins by acknowledging and accepting the difference.

Most people who are uncomfortable with unclothed bodies missed this step and erroneously think that sex and any kind of nudity go together. If they see nudity, they selfishly think sexual thoughts instead of beauty and respect for physical differences. If they hear about sex, they think nudity rather than the caring warmth being shared between two people who are being intimate. Of all the developed countries, our society is the most uncomfortable with non-sexual nudity, and in part because of this narrow-minded logic, we have the society with the highest sex crime rate.

Although nudity and sex can and do go together within a caring, committed relationship, unclothed or nude bodies do not and should not always be equated with sex. This type of one-sided thinking is what skews our society's views of the opposite sex and contributes significantly to crimes against women in our society. It also gives sex the major focus in a relationship, at the expense of the more important aspects of support for your partner's personal growth, commitment, and working through difficult issues. In our fast-paced society, one needs to understand and know there is a difference between sex and nudity in order to pay attention to the important and long-standing aspects of relationships.

2.) Continue age-appropriate sexuality conversations throughout their growing years.

Openly talk about sex with children and teenagers of all ages. For your children, it may be identifying different body parts, including the genitals. For school-age children, it can involve how babies are made and how people love each other more than anybody else before being sexually close or intimate. For pre-teens, it can be more detailed information on how body parts work, sexually transmitted diseases, birth control, and the importance of commitment before sharing sexual hugs. For teenagers, it can be age-appropriate touch in sexual relationships, balancing couple and friendship group time, and comparing different kids' and parents' views on sexual contact and love. Find answers together, ask even when it sounds dumb, and judge together the healthy and unhealthy kinds of touch that are viewed in movies, television, and the media.

Once this step has been done only a few times, it becomes comfortable. The talks can be short by making only a few comments, or more involved as children and teenagers become accustomed to these occasional talks and ask more questions; the idea that the parent is not the expert, but can find answers with their kids is also very helpful. It is important to commonly and respectfully use words like penis, vagina, and sexual intercourse when talking with kids. Comfort and respect are slowly developed by using these actual words instead of slang or pet names when talking about body parts or sexuality.

Remembering to listen first when kids are responding to a question or giving their opinions on sexuality increases and solidifies parent and child communication. If children or teenagers say something that you disagree with, ask them how they came to their opinion before you calmly, and without trying to change their minds, express your opinion. No topic or issue necessarily needs to be resolved in one discussion. It can evolve, change, and be brought to a fuller understanding throughout their thinking process and several short conversations. It is a better parent who keeps calm while helping their kids explore and learn in their own unique ways than it is for a parent to pressure or require their kids to memorize parental beliefs.

3.) Give hugs, don't ask for them.

When interacting with your children, give hugs, don't ask for them. For example, "Come here, I'd like to give you a hug," or "I forgot to give you a morning hug." Avoid saying, "Come here, I need a hug," or "Okay, give your mom or dad a hug and kiss now." Kids who receive hugs feel good, free, and nurtured. Kids who are asked for hugs or kisses typically end up feeling burdened, pressured to caretake, or responsible for their parents' happiness. Enjoy affection that is initiated by your children, as well as respond immediately when they need or ask for a hug; however, parents must view themselves as the nurturer. Kids are not equals; they are the receivers, and parents are the givers. Parents need to hug, hold, and touch children all the way through their teenage years. Play with them and talk with them more than you watch television.

"Play," as defined by mutual, spontaneous interactions between two or more people, has been lost in our society. It seems the only two accepted forms of play left are dancing and laughing. Sports are close, but are no longer really play. Big people have taken over and organized them. There's a goal in mind: winning. Real play has no goal of winning or losing, beginning or ending. It just happens. It is two or more people enjoying each other, the moment, and whatever spontaneous game they just invented—maybe never to be played again, but fun and lively in the moment.

Play isn't teasing or making fun of someone. It's not plotting a joke on another. It's definitely not parents organizing and taking over a sport their kids like to play. "Play," defined by Webster, is "to move lightly, engage, or take part in trifle, with another person or object. To pretend, make believe, or behave in an affected or dramatic manner." It is also mutual, spontaneous, and honest. People who play can talk about or exaggerate anything to interact with another. It may last a few seconds or occur over many hours. It may involve acting like you tripped or ran into a door. It may be tickling each other and trying not to laugh. Or it may be sticking your finger into a close-eyed friend's mouth and pulling it out before they bite down. Its only purpose is to engage the two, or three, into enjoying each other, the moment, and strengthening their trust and closeness. Children and teenagers who play with their parents not only trust them, but can be more present and attentive in serious moments because they have experienced the opposite. When parents are consistent, their playfulness develops trust and also it indirectly benefits more serious conversations.

4.) Celebrate their coming-of-age.

Plan and acknowledge with a gift and a family celebration when daughters have their first period and when sons have their 12th or 13th birthday. Honor and give congratulations on their coming-ofage and new maturity. Give flowers, prepare a big dinner, or go to a show. Schedule a camping trip, a day at the lake, or an overnight out of town. Tailor the celebration and activity to your teenager's type of personality and style. This is a time of change for teenagers. They are starting to leave behind younger days, and beginning to learn and develop their own identities and independence. Respectfully and joyously celebrating and honoring this bittersweet time for them is deeply affirming.

Throughout time, many cultures, including Native American, have celebrated and honored their children when they becoming young women and men. Because our American society has lost this important tradition is no reason to neglect it within our families. Our young people need this kind of respectful acknowledgement and support, not only as another life transition, but also as uniquely strengthening for being a female or a male. Our society does little to honor and respectfully uphold male and female differences unless it's provocatively sexualized. By families honoring and supporting a boy or girl as they become physically mature, they not only cuts through society's negative sexual images of being male or female, it also nurtures a profound individual strength within our young people.

In families where these childhood and teenage life transitions are supported and celebrated, kids develop mature, strong personalities, and kids who have well-adjusted personalities tend to avoid trouble and find success in their lives.

5.) Fathers: Treating daughters as a person first, and sons as someone to nurture.

Daughters

Talk to your daughter as an individual by acknowledging her endeavors and personality more then her prettiness. Honor her decisions more than you give her advice. Apologize when you are wrong and allow her the independence to make her own mistakes. Listen to her anger respectfully; let her fix things and put no limits on her dreams. Support and speak up for her when she asks, and stay in the background when she wants to try something for herself. Give her as much independence as you would have expected for yourself at her age. If your daughter is raised with this kind of respect, support, and listening, she will accept no less in any of her male relationships.

It's important to remember that usually a daughter's first experience with a male in her life is with her father. If that experience is one filled with caring affection and respect for her as a person first and consistent support for her independence, rather than her being a certain sex with limitations, then she becomes a strong individual. That is provided that her father continues this kind of positive relationship, then she grows into a confident and mature young woman. Frequently, fathers pull back and become uncomfortable with touch or affection once their daughters reach young womanhood. This is an unconscious, yet significant mistake. It is the first of many societal steps that can unknowingly put girls into a sexualized category of importance. Most fathers don't want to view or categorize their daughters in such a way; however, in their attempt to ignore or avoid her physical changes, discomfort leads to less affection.

Often daughters feel slighted by their father's discomfort and more reserved behavior. They begin to feel that something is wrong with them or that because of their physical changes they now have to reserve themselves for sexual encounters. This subtle change that fathers unconsciously fall into toward their daughters has far-reaching negative affects on the purpose of her personal sexuality, the way she relates to the opposite sex, and her feminine image.

Daughters need their father's spontaneity and healthy affection throughout their growing and developing, including the teenager years. A father's on-going healthy touch reminds a daughter that she is special and loved as a person first. Her sexuality is part of her, but not the most important part. By experiencing appropriate affection throughout all her growing years, a daughter will be instilled with a natural ability to balance healthy affection and responsibly decide on the timing of intimate sexual touch within her boyfriend relationships.

When daughters are pre-school age, holding, rocking, and playing need to be priorities for fathers. In kindergarten through second grade, daughters need individual special time from their father to play, be listened to, and affectionately held. Third through fifth graders need their dads to continue individual special time for listening, supporting her newly forming perceptions of her world, and having fun with her and her friends. Sixth through eighth graders need their dads to support and accept their quickly changing minds, compliment her on accomplishments as much as her prettiness, continue to give more privileges than her younger siblings, and daily healthy affection. Ninth and tenth grade daughters need their fathers to support them for their friendship group, their expanding ideas, affection only at home if that's their comfort level, and approval of their boyfriend choices. Eleventh and twelfth grade daughters need their fathers to stand back and allow them to make many of their personal and friendship decisions, trust them with the car in snowy conditions, allow them to change the car oil, and go on trips with friends.

Daughters who experience continuous support, listening, and affection from their fathers tend to have a more self-accepting body image, confidence in themselves and their opinions in the presence of males, and a mature outlook on their world. These stages in the father and daughter relationship vary among families, but the common denominators are listening, supporting, slowly increasing trust and privileges, and affection.

Sons

Talk to your son, knowing he needs your gentle side as often as your strength. Watch his sports activities for his fun without focusing on coaching or your private expectations. Let him see you always treat your wife as an equal, and allow him to witness you listen, talk respectfully, and compromise with her. Be more of a doer of activities with him, rather than a talker of how he ought to be. Include quiet times together, hear him out when he's upset, and allow him to cry. Give affection for fun, but also for support. Never hold back from hugging him, and tell him you're proud when he helps another. Ask him about his friendships more than his sports, and always be there to put a bandage on his cuts.

A boy's strength and toughness comes from a close, well-rounded relationship with his father. This includes affection, wrestling, tickling, nurturing hugs when he's hurt, remembering what he likes and dislikes, and respectful, consistent consequences when he chooses negative behavior. It does not come from coaching him to play a sport better, looking disappointedly at him when he has tears, or changing the entire family schedule to work around his sports schedule.

Strength and resilience comes from a father who can view the world through his son's eyes and respond accordingly. It does not come from a father who suddenly decides at age four that his son no longer needs his blankie or pacifier and throws it out. Rather, it comes from a father who tells his son at age four or five that he can have his blankie, a pacifier, or thumb while in his bedroom or watching television. As his son becomes six or seven, he can tell him to use his blankie or thumb only in his bedroom. This kind of approach teaches a boy appropriate personal boundaries, while at the same time experiencing his father's unconditional support. Lessons and life changes that are learned through this type of supportive guidance as opposed to reactive shaming raises strong and caring boys. Words alone cannot teach or give strength. Only when words are combined with caring actions can a boy follow solidly in his father's footsteps.

In order to continue this strengthening type of parenting for grade-school age boys, fathers need to respectfully listen to their son's daily activities, support him when he is giving or caring toward his sisters, and hug and hold and affectionately play with him. Boys at this age need a lot of time with their fathers spent in playing games, reading, watching movies, and special time before bed.

Teenage boys need their fathers to be available for rides to friends' houses, listening to his newly forming opinions, and avoid being in a coaching role. At this age a son needs his father for a behind-thescenes personal supporter while he ventures out with his friends, rather than focusing on sports and coaching which take away from the more important role as his nurturer. It is more beneficial to compliment him on his positives when he asks how you thought the game went than it is to coach him on what needs improvement.

It's also important for fathers to remember that sports do not teach a son how to get along with others and be a team player. A boy learns how to get along with others and take turns from his father and mother early in life. Sports merely becomes another place where a boy can use the personal skills his parents have given him. If a boy hasn't learned about giving, taking turns, and teamwork before he plays sports, it's unlikely and rare that he will learn it from others where he is competing for a spot on the team and is not involved in a personal relationship.

Older teenage sons need their fathers to be calm, well-directed in their own life, respectfully equal with their partner, available for talks, and actively listening and expressing trust in his son's decisions and life choices. Affirming a close connection with a son happens less frequently in older teenagers, but should always be given when the chance arises. An established bond will keep a father and son genuinely connected over the years if a father consistently shows love and respect for their personal differences.

When a son is allowed to see and experience a complete picture of his father's moods, behaviors, assertiveness, and gentleness, he can become a well-adjusted boy and young man. By allowing this kind of closeness, fathers instill a personal stability which their sons can use to adjust and succeed in various situations they will encounter. Sons raised in this way have the ability to use their developing strength or their nurturing gentleness in appropriate situations.

6.) Mothers: Treating sons as kids, not equals, and setting your daughters free.

Sons

Give your son a smile when he is respectful; confront and give him a consequence when he is rude or discounting. Play catch with him when he is young and teach him to do his own wash. Show support for his mindful endeavors as often as his physical activities. Let him see your confidence show through your personality rather than how you look or how much you weigh. Use your steady, calm strength when he tries to intimidate; don't be afraid to give him a consequence the next day after you've had time to think, and always hug him with your head above his.

Boys respect their mother if she does what she says and if she acts like she talks. Mothers who put on in front of other people or pout when they're mad instead of using words or directives are often made fun of by their sons. Mothers gain their son's trust and respect primarily by demonstrating personal strength in various situations. These include talking as an equal with a spouse, being yourself in the presence of others, pulling him aside in front of his friends if that's where he has chosen to be disrespectful, and saying you're proud of him when he helps someone younger.

Affection, play, and hugs are important if they are given, rather than asked for. This is a subtle difference, but necessary because over the years asking for hugs can make a son feel like the stronger one, and a son who feels stronger than his mother can become superficially inflated. This makes many sons approach relationships with women as if he should be catered to. However, a son who has a strong mother often has more equal and self-respecting relationships with the opposite sex. He has no need to prove himself or obtain something he was emotionally missing from his mother, so his girlfriend relationships are comfortable, real, and long-lasting. Sons of strong mothers also develop a closeness that can be appreciated throughout the years of his adult life.

Daughters

Support your daughter's independence and let her voice be strong. Allow her to choose beyond your expectations and show her that coming into womanhood is special and strong. Let her see you talk to your husband with confidence, equality, and fair compromising rather than asking permission. Give her outdoor chores, know that her disagreeing and anger are for personal independence, not dislike, and save adult topics for your friends. Feel comfortable having some adult activities outside of parenting, supportively listen to her dreams, and allow her to become self-sufficient.

Because I have never been in this type of relationship, I can only comment on what I've seen work between my wife and our daughter and the mothers and daughters I've been privileged to work with in therapy. Mothers and daughters who are appropriately close are where mothers support their daughters' different ideals and opinions, play with and hug their daughters, and slowly allow their daughters to find independence without guilt. These mothers and daughters may argue or disagree, but they do it respectfully and without put downs. They may cry together and have apologies, but it is done with the mother taking responsibility for her own issues and allowing her daughter the time to recognize her own need for improvement.

In situations where a mother did not experience appropriate closeness with her mother or father, attending her own individual therapy to heal her past feelings can dramatically improve a relationship with her daughter. Mothers who have the courage to resolve their past feelings are giving an internal gift to their daughters in the form of a current, emotionally healthy relationship with them. It is these kinds of courageous mothers who after doing their own work can sit back and watch with joy as their daughters grow and learn to succeed within their young world.

7.) Giving and volunteering to those in need.

Although not specifically sexual in nature, we as a society do not live in a vacuum, and therefore giving and volunteering are an integral part of a child's and teenager's emotional development. To be pulled out of one's own life to give to another who is in need lends a necessary perspective to their world view. Without it, they are bound to the narrow-mindedness that accompanies a focus only on themselves. With it, different perspectives and doors are open to all of the world's peoples, situations, and the big picture of how society works. In our day and age, this is an absolute necessity for anyone expecting to grasp the world and responsibly fit themselves into it.

Most volunteering can begin comfortably and lightly at a young age. Taking young children shopping for a Santa Anonymous toy during the winter holidays is a good first step. Grade-school-age children can accompany parents while chaperoning a field trip for children at a women's shelter. Volunteering for community or church organized food shelf drives or Meals-on-Wheels are appropriate for middle school kids. High school teenagers could work at a hospital's volunteer services department, tutoring of children in after school programs, or peer counseling programs.

The important aspect is helping or giving their time to another human being. When kids are young, it doesn't have to be a major commitment. It just needs to be ongoing so that it becomes a part of their lives and their growing years. Assisting, volunteering, and helping others is an important step in raising well-rounded kids.

To uphold sexuality in these seven ways of respecting it with our words and honoring it in our actions is a legacy beyond generations. It will nurture and strengthen children and teenagers well past their young life and carry them to their highest levels of confidence and personal awareness. No matter how uncomfortable it might make parents feel initially or how much practice it takes with a spouse, prior to enacting this approach the only choice for giving strength and maturity to our kids is consistently doing it.

The Healthy Sexuality Series for Families: A Complete Sex Education Outline for Families

1.) "Opening"

Everyone in the family takes a turn to say where they first learned about sex. Was it comfortable or uncomfortable, open dialogue, or under the table? Allow laughing and silliness to be present. The more sex is talked about in respectful, caring ways, the more that will subside. Parents go first.

2.) "Comment"

Everyone states if this will be comfortable because they are used to talking about sex, or state if they are uncomfortable because they usually never talk about sex so openly and in a caring way. Also, discuss only two of the topics at one sitting. Wait up to a week and discuss two more.

3.) Male Body

One family member uses a chart and describes the reproductive and sexual parts of the male body. Be sure to include the penis, testicles, scrotum, vas deferens, prostate, cowper's glands, semenal vesicle, epidydimus, and how they work during sex, how they change through puberty and life, and use pictures of unclothed males of all ages—0 through age 85. After the male body is presented, all family members ask at least one question about the male body and any family member can answer. Be open to several right, or workable answers.

4.) Female Body

One family member uses a chart and describes the reproductive and sexual parts of the female body. Include the vagina, clitoris, labia, hymen, cervix, uterus, fallopian tubes, ovaries, and sexual functioning as well as non-sexual functions. Include changes in puberty, menopause, and aging in the discussion. After the female body is presented, all family members ask at least one question and any family member can answer. Again, be open to several different, or workable answers.

5.) Sexual Terms

One family member reads and explains one sexual word or term at a time. Include these basic words and terms: sexual intercourse, masturbation, orgasm, oral sex, homosexuality, puberty, menopause, menstrual cycle, douche, and others you may want to add. Allow slang terms to be stated, along with the importance of the respectful proper term. Focus on how sexual intercourse can take place within a loving, intimate relationship, and how it can occur but doesn't feel right outside of a loving, committed relationship. Describe the feelings within a loving relationship and the lack of positive feelings in a superficial relationship. All family members ask questions and any family member can answer.

6.) Sexually Transmitted Diseases

A family member uses a chart that lists five to seven genital diseases. Explain how these types of diseases began. The two prevailing theories are men having sex with domesticated animals in early European history, and men and women prior to the discovery of germs not being aware of washing themselves. This caused much bacteria build-up on people's genitals, and therefore diseases spread. Describe each disease separately and explain whether it's a virus or bacteria, its symptoms, and how it is treated. Include herpes, A.I.D.S., crabs, gonorrhea, syphilis, and chlamydia. After presenting, each family member asks a question and anyone can answer and have open discussion.

7.) Birth Control

A family member presents a chart showing numerous birth control methods. Make it interesting by actually displaying a condom or pills and describe how they work. Include tubal ligation, vasectomy, the pill, condoms, diaphragm and contraceptive foams, intra-uterine devices (I.U.D.), hormone injections or implants, cervical caps, sponge, female condoms, and rhythm method. Discuss the percentages for avoiding pregnancy with each method and where various items can be purchased. All family members ask at least one question and let the conversation flow, with natural lulls in the dialogue.

8.) Healthy and unhealthy sexuality

A family member organizes two poster boards, one labeled "healthy touch" and the other labeled "unhealthy touch,"' numerous magazines, pictures, scissors and tape. Explain that healthy sexuality is touch or intimate affection between two people where caring, mutual, respectful, and warm feelings are present. Explain that unhealthy touch is just a showiness, a physical turn on, or a dominating attitude over another. Have all family members cut out pictures from the magazines and tape them onto the healthy posterboard or the unhealthy posterboard. Hold the collages within everyone's view and ask where each of the different types of touches can be found. Talk about the curiosity of the unhealthy showiness compared to the personal warmth and deep feeling of healthy touch. Have an open position regarding all types of caring relationships, and emphasize that a person's gender does not matter as significantly as their feelings and intentions. Ask if there is love, respect, and caring between the two that make it healthy, or is there only a physicalness and showiness that makes it just skin-deep, and therefore unhealthy?

If questions arise regarding what certain religious stances are regarding same sex relationships, explore different beliefs. Also, include a definition of intolerance, narrow-minded interpretations, and how humans use their own insecurities to make others comply with their beliefs. Be open to everyone's opinions and decisions, and remember, the definition of healthy touch is deep, respectful, personal feelings, and the definition of unhealthy touch is surface showiness where the intent is just for a physical turn-on.

9.) Age Appropriate Sexual Touch

Another family member guides everyone to make their own chart. On the top make four columns and put the headings: Parents, Community/Church, Friends, and Self. Down the left side of the chart, list the following labels under the title of age; boyfriend or girlfriend, holding hands, kissing on cheek, hugging and kissing on lips, touching each other's chest or breasts, touching each other's genitals, sexual intercourse, masturbation, life long commitment/ marriage.

Name

Age	Parents	Church	Friends	Self
Boyfriend or girlfriend				
Holding hands				
Kissing on cheek				
Hugging & kissing on lips				
Touching each other's chest or breasts				
Touching each other's genitals				
Sexual Intercourse				
Masturbation				
Life-long commitment/marriage				

In the boxes, fill in the age when you believe that kind of touch is appropriate.

Each family member privately fills out his or her own chart. Keep in mind that the touch is within a caring relationship as you fill in the boxes with the age you believe the listed behavior is healthy and appropriate. Try to answer parents, church, and friends before filling in self-answers.

After everyone has completed his or her charts, take turns sharing. The leading family member on this topic facilitates the discussion, reminding family members that it is an open discussion and not a time to correct or put down anyone's self answers. Questions are okay, lessons in life or trying to change someone's mind is not.

10.) Positive Sexuality

The whole family takes part in this final topic by giving their definition of why sex is positive—how it can always be healthy and how to keep it positive. Remember that real beauty is in caring feelings, deep meaning is in the love between two people, and true freedom is found within long-lasting relationships and the commitments between people. Although this is a structured format for teaching sex education, it does not need to be strictly adhered to. Parents need to judge how much to say during one discussion, how long to wait in between talks, and how detailed to get, depending on age. The important aspect is that these kinds of inclusive talks ought to begin at home and at a young age. They can be light and short, but periodically talking about sex education issues is a necessity and a tantamount responsibility for parents who care about raising well-adjusted kids.

Breaking Barriers

Breaking through our society's negative presentations of sexuality is a significant step in the authentic development of our children and teenagers. These unhealthy societal presentations have actually become barriers to our kids' personal development. They include:

- allowing boys to say they are better than girls or going first in line because they are a boy
- being silent after watching a sexual television commercial with children present,
- giving priority and more attendance to a son's sports activities rather than balancing time with a daughter's sports activities,
- having daughters do indoor home chores and sons do outdoor home chores,
- making sports television viewing a frequent and primary form of entertainment.

These are all common ways of doing things; however, if they are not changed all of the negative messages of the media are being invited into our children's minds and life experience. However, when kids are raised with the rich and respectful experiences of sex education talks, seeing healthy sexuality books around the house, and witness their parents comfortably and appropriately changing clothes or using the bathroom, children and teenagers come to know a different way. When kids actually live differently than what the media presents, they can confidently make the choice to remain with what's real in life, approach the opposite sex as equals, and even honor their differences. These types of reality-based experiences and openness in their upbringing enables and encourages girls and boys to become compatible, rather than competitive.

Openness is important because when boys grow up and never see a female body in a non-sexual situation, too many boys begin to view women as primarily for sexual purposes. Likewise, when girls grow up and never see a male body in a non-sexual situation, too many girls begin to view men as primarily for sexual purposes. For a significant number of boys and girls, these sexual-purpose beliefs get translated into boys trying to dominate women and girls trying to look attractive and desirable. This is a formula for disrespect and abuse, and can only be changed by the caring and respectful openness in the upbringing of our children and teenagers.

Sometimes kids will bring up a sexual topic, and with an open attitude by the parent, the conversation may go something like this:

"Dad, what does 'dick' mean?"

"Oh, did you hear that word today?"

"Yeah, Johnny said it when we were playing in his snow fort."

"How did he say it?"

"Carl wanted to play with us and Johnny said, 'He's a dick, don't let him in.'"

"Oh, I see. Well, what's your guess? What do you think it means?"

"I don't know, but it's something to do with going to the bathroom, because when Johnny said it he stood up like he was going to the bathroom."

"That's very good, son. You're right, it does have something to do with going to the bathroom. Remember that our penis is what we go to the bathroom with?"

"Yeah."

"Well, that's what 'dick' means."

"A penis?"

"Yes, but I have to tell you something else about the word 'dick'."

"What?"

"It's a mean thing to call your penis or someone else. It's just like if you called someone stupid. Or if you called your hand dumb because you didn't throw the ball right where you wanted it to go."

"You mean like in baseball when I throw it over the first baseman's head?"

"That's right. So, anything else you wanted to say about penis or dick?"

"No, but can I say that word?"

"I'm glad you asked that question. What do you think?"

"No, not really."

"That's how I feel, son. I respect you and myself, so I try not to say mean things about parts of my body, or toward someone else either."

"Me too, Dad."

"Hey, let's go play catch and see where your nice strong hand throws the ball."

The conversation doesn't need to be heavy or long. It just needs to allow you to hear out your child, express how you feel, and give an example of saying things respectfully. Demonstrate the way for appropriateness and respect and allow them to make their own decisions.

Other times, a parent has to open up the topic and a talk with a teenager may go something like this:

"Son, I want to ask you a quick question about a sex thing."

"Come on, Dad, I'm not going to talk about sex with you."

"I know, but how about just your opinion on one thing?"

"Depends on what it is."

"Well, I'm just wondering what kids your age—you know, in your grade at school—do if their boyfriend or girlfriend wants to go all the way sexually, and you or another person doesn't want to."

"I don't know, I've never been in a situation like that. Why are you asking me such a weird question, anyway?"

"Only because I care about what you might have to go through some day."

"It's not like that happens all the time, you know."

"Oh, I know, but what could someone your age do if it did, just by chance, happen?"

"I don't know, just tell them you don't want to."

"And what would your girlfriend's reaction be, and friends who would hear about it as school?"

"I really wouldn't care what friends said; it's mine and her business, not theirs."

"Yeah, but if they heard about it, would they bug you about not going that far?"

"Some people would, but they're not really my friends."

"And what about your girlfriend? What would her reaction be?"

"If she really wanted to go farther, she might get mad, but we would keep talking about it until something worked out."

"Would you ever talk about it with me if you felt in a tight spot?"

"No, probably my friends first, and then my sister, because she's older and she knows a lot about this kind of stuff."

"Good for you, son. I'm glad you have some friends and your sister to talk to. If you ever change your mind about talking to me, or you can't talk with your friends or sister, I'm very comfortable talking to you if you'd like."

"Probably not, but thanks, Dad."

The conversation doesn't need to solve anything or pressure him to talk in the future. Simply addressing the topic comfortably is positive. If a teenager even talks like this to a parent, that's open communication. With teenagers, they have to be in the mood, parents have to respect their growing privacy, and listening to their opinions on other topics is paramount to a good relationship.

Parenting Beyond

One of the most significant ways for parents to increase their children's knowledge base, broaden their communication skills, and develop their maturity is by parenting beyond the media's norms. Typically, children and teenagers see only a skewed and glitzy side of life from the media. This occurs because the media's purpose is to attract and hold one's attention. The media is not interested in teaching our kids about real life, rather, their focus is about their image and their product. And the media does this by keeping kids off balance with confusing or fast-paced scenes or messages and constantly bombarding them with new and different things.

The only effective way to counter this "blitz of glitz" by the media and to really educate our kids is to parent them with more openness than what they're seeing in the media. I call this "parenting beyond" and anything short of more openness than the media allows the media to maintain the upper hand. Having kids spend less time exposed to various media is only a part of the answer. The bigger part of the answer, regardless of how much media exposure kids have, is more openness to what the media is constantly and manipulatively alluding too. "Parenting beyond" includes matching words and actions. For example, when a family views a movie with several sexual scenes, a caring parent will comment on it after the show. Even a short discussion on the movie's main message and its ludicrous use of provocative or shallow sex can be enough to change kids naivety to awareness. Also, if a teenager begins asking questions about relationships, sex, or other personal topics, a parent going beyond will turn off the television or put down the newspaper and listen. They will share personal experiences as much as they expect their teenager to share, and parenting beyond means always having available around the home,

magazines, and picture books that deal with sex in appropriate and caring ways. These should include non-sexual pictures of unclothed bodies and other pictures of loving people in more intimate situations.

Children and teenagers who do not experience openness or parents whose words and actions don't match are usually confused. These include parents who say nothing about sexuality and sexual relations, yet watch movie after movie with numerous sexual messages. On one hand, they are uncomfortable talking about sex; however, on the other hand they thoroughly enjoy watching sexual movies. A child or teenager seeing their parents act this way automatically assume that watching sexually alluring media is acceptable, but talking about it is not. These kids become perfectly groomed to accept how the media presents life.

Children and teenagers who experience parenting beyond the media's shallow norms tend to frown at sexually provocative and confusing advertising. Because of their developing awareness, they view such media presentations as weird or silly. They have grown accustomed to straightforward and open sexuality talks so that the media's narrowly focused presentations are below their maturity level. In situations where naive or inexperienced kids are held captive by the media's provocative presentations, kids who experience openness with their parents can comfortably get past the silliness of such advertising. In their lives, they have come to know and understand a more complete and real side of life than the media presents because their upbringing is replete with caring, respectful, and open sexuality discussions.

Walking the Talk

Regarding teenagers, parents need to avoid falling into the "I'll tell them how to do it" trap. A parent will never really help, lead or guide a teenager through such personal issues as sexuality unless they have come to some understanding by also growing themselves. A parent must resolve their own discomforts through adult talk and role-playing practice as well as their own emotional baggage before they'll ever have an acceptable voice with a teenager. Teenagers will know if you as a parent know experientially or actually believe what you're saying because you currently live it, or if you're just saying the words in a feeble attempt to parent them with a lesson-in-life lecture.

Teenagers don't need and can't really use lectures on how life should be. They need talks that are real and personable—talks with their parents where they believe they have been listened to and understood. A parent can best help their teenager by showing that they are on the same side as their kids. The basic assumption is "we" and "together," not "us" against "them." In order to foster a "we" and "together" perspective, parents need to listen, ask questions about their teenager's statements in order to better understand them, and then share their own thoughts. Listening to a teenager's feelings or thoughts before sharing your own perspective is one of the best ways to ensure openness and therefore ongoing closeness with a teenager.

A Strong Stance

One way in which parents can internally feel confident about addressing sexuality in positive ways is by writing their beliefs similar to a mission statement. Parents don't need to frequently discuss their moral view or lecture their kids on its details, but merely having one kids are aware of is beneficial. A strong and informed belief concerning the media and the way it deals with sexuality might sound like the following:

"Do what you want within the guidelines of the law, but until you put more substance in your advertising in the area of mutually caring relationships among men and women, I will not support or purchase your product. In addition, I will take back my responsibility as a parent by teaching and showing my kids what you are alluding to in your provocative presentations. This will include everything I can find that will show them intimacy in caring relationships, respectful and healthy sexuality pictures of the human body, that the best relationships are those that last, how to relate to another human being as a person first, and their gender second. I will do all of this with an attitude of openness, fun, and confidence because I know that what I'm doing by talking and showing my kids complete sexuality is proper and right. It instills lifelong maturity and confidence. It opens a world of knowledge to them which goes beyond what the media presents, and it makes it possible for them to take a stand for what they believe is right. I will also do this open talk with other adults who are comfortable, and again, we will do it with fun, confidence, and a sense of humor. We will also be aware and open to our kids' questions, differences, and creative ways of doing things."

Our children and teenagers have only us to look up to for those important aspects of sexuality that the media only tease and allude to. If we do not teach and show our kids the bigger picture, they will, and do, turn to the media for life. In our society, kids will always be exposed to at least parts of the media, but they don't have a chance to put it into perspective or come through it if we don't have something greater and more complete to offer them. As parents, our complete openness and appropriate actions are the only truths we have to captivate them beyond the fun and exciting things they view in the media.

The more sexually respectful material is available and out in the open for our kids, the less effect the sexually provocative media will have on them. However, this open approach is initially uncomfortable and is often criticized. This criticism arises because we have been raised in a society where nudity has always been equated with sex. However, in reality there is an appropriate and respectful difference between an unclothed human body and sex, but until parents make it apparent in their words and actions, our children and teenagers will not have the aptitude to get beyond the one-sided presentations of the media.

Creating Strong Cores Rather Than Empty Shells

Some parents have fears that by openly teaching and completely educating kids on sexuality issues it will encourage them or give them permission to become sexually active. In my 21 years of practicing therapy with children and teenagers I have not found this assumption to be true. On the contrary, I have witnessed kids with openly presented knowledge and complete sexuality information regularly making sound, important decisions regarding their personal safety and relationship choices. There are numerous studies that have also demonstrated this finding to be true.[17] This research has shown that teenagers with sexuality knowledge tend to consider their choices more completely, and with communication prior to becoming sexually active they often delay intimate activity when compared to their peers and are more likely to utilize birth control methods if they do decide to become sexually intimate. Although we as parents may prefer that our teenagers do not become sexually active, giving them our support and attention in talks about personal sexuality, and sharing our feelings rather than figures and statistics affords them a safe place to make a good decision.

Teenagers who are raised in this kind of supportive openness are well-equipped to deal with difficult issues and peer pressure. Teenagers who do not experience parental openness and education on sexuality issues are usually naive kids waiting or looking for anyone or any place to learn. Their façade of control or memorized rules of behavior is a thin shell to their empty and truth-seeking cores. It is a travesty for parents to not inform and openly educate their own children and teenagers for fear of them making different choices. The cost of a teenager not knowing complete sexuality information is often greater than the effects of learning from their mistakes. The biggest cost to a naive teenager is learning about sexuality in piecemeal ways, incompletely, and from the media. Over the course of many years that could have been used for healthy and relationship respectful sexuality knowledge, these uninformed teenagers become perfect consumers of the media's

17   Kirby, D., National Guidelines Task Force, Grunseit, A., and Kippax, S.

superficial influence. A teenager's only real hope of creating a strong core instead of a sponge-like center just waiting to be filled in by the media and incomplete peer information is parents who are willing to openly and frequently talk, act, and listen to a different and more open way concerning sexuality.

C.) The Positive Change

Dispelling myths and moving forward

What children and teenagers experience in their own families, in terms of caring sexuality openness, determines how successfully they can navigate past the media's provocativeness. More importantly, their open family experience regarding sexuality promotes the personal capacity to find success, safety, and trust in many of their life relationships. When families deal openly and respectfully with sexual topics, their kids also become well-versed on many other personal topics and respectfully confident in their demeanor. Unfortunately, kids who do not experience family openness on personal sexuality topics are at a disadvantage when encountering and trying to make sense of our sexualized society. It hits too fast and too frequently for these uninformed kids to manage their emotions when they have a weak foundation in sexuality knowledge.

The chance to give knowledge and confidence to kids is either taken and acted upon or lost by parents during the growing years. Avoidance or infrequent talks lead to stagnation. The media and uninformed peers will always be present, but their negative sway is dissipated and kept in perspective by kids who have been raised in families with complete sexuality openness and respect. Their knowledge base is more complete and their experiences too broad for these outside influences to have a significant impact or affect on them.

Although some parents believe that avoiding sexual topics or minimal talks about sexuality is the safest approach, in my practice with teenagers and their families I have found the opposite to be true. Uninformed or naïve kids appear to struggle more with the adult world where they do not have an open and personal connection. They also seem to have difficulty trusting adults and authority, and generally are more prone to acting impulsively. Well-informed and sexually knowledgeable kids seem to have a natural confidence with others, knowingly articulate their opinions, and can calmly listen to all sides of an issue before making their own decisions. This air or feeling of independence and sureness in knowledgeable kids naturally overshadows and leaves kids behind who are not well-versed in personal topics. It is a subtle, yet noticeable difference that becomes more apparent as kids become teenagers. The anxieties and doubtfulness of ill-informed kids is no match next to the knowledge and confidence of kids who have been raised in comfortably open families regarding the personal issues of sexuality.

Parents who become capable in sexuality communication with their kids help themselves and their kids avoid the pitfalls and long-range negative effects of our society's sexual assumptions. Some of the more commonly held sexual opinions or myths include:

False—The more sex information kids learn, the more sexually active they become.

In specific studies and in my practice I have discovered that kids who learn complete sex education and can talk openly and frequently about the topic with their parents are not necessarily prone to becoming sexually active. On the contrary, I have found that kids who have complete knowledge and comfortably talk about sex within their families tend to think about sex before they may decide to experience it within a caring relationship. Their decisions are well-informed and they usually talk about it, to some extent, with their parents. Although these are kids who tend to have strong relationships and openness within their families, even kids without comfortable and frequently open communication with their parents tend to make safer decisions about sexual intimacy if they have experienced some sexuality openness. It may be something as simple as deciding to use birth control or holding off until dating the same person for an extended period of time; however, their choices are more self-directed than kids who lack knowledge and openness with a parent.

There are exceptions to these healthy, more knowledgeable patterns, but often these exceptions occur where open communication has broken down or sexuality is no longer talked about as frequently. Resentment and anger build when personal topics are not talked about or where parents do not respectfully listen to their teenagers, and therefore the impulse to act out in a rebellious way is higher.

Once a child or teenager is comfortable due to their parent's openness, some kids will talk openly and feel comfortable asking personal questions. Others will be hesitant and ask questions or allude to topics by indirectly asking about a friend's situation. Or they may use the, "What if I did this or that?" type of questioning. The key to open communication is no matter what style a child or teenager uses, a parent needs to be a listener first, ask good questions about their kid's opinion, and then express their own opinion. It's important to remember that a decision or consensus does not need to be reached in any one conversation. These are important, personal topics and moments with kids, and naturally coming to a decision or forming a value takes place over several talks and a lot of time. A parent who listens and asks questions before giving an opinion will gradually experience openness and a strengthened relationship with their child or teenager.

Communication with a resistant teenager may sound like this:

"Mom, I don't like talking about sex stuff with you. It's more with my friends that I can talk about this kind of stuff."

"I know, Sara, so let's keep it short, but this stuff is important."

"Mom…"

"I know, come on. We'll each just ask one question and then I'll drop you off at Molly's house."

"Oh, Mom…"

"Okay, do you want to go first or should I?"

"You—this is stupid."

"Okay, I've always wondered if kids in your grade talk about sex stuff with guys they're going out with?"

"Depends on the guy—and the girl—if she really wants to or not."

"Oh, and what's kind of the norm, would you say?"

"Mom, that's two questions!"

"Okay, you got me, you go next."

"I don't know, there's nothing I want to ask you."

"Come on, it can be about anything, even when I was younger."

"Really?"

"Yeah."

"Okay, when did you first kiss a boyfriend?"

"You mean a quick peck, or some real long kissing?"

"Some real long kissing."

"It was with this guy I really liked. We were in 10th grade."

"10th grade? Isn't that kind of old?"

"Well, not for me at the time. Why, is it younger now when kids have long kisses?"

"Yes, even by 8th grade now."

"Oh, times have changed. What do you think about long kisses in 8th grade?"

"It's fine, if you really like each other."

"That's a good thing you said, Sara. I like the way you think about things."

"Yeah, can we go now, Mom?"

"Sure, I'll grab my purse and meet you in the car."

Sometimes it will be tense like in this example, but it's a start, and it can lead to more talks. Sara may not always like it, and the mom may not always like bringing the topic up, but there is a closeness forming that can be built on again and again. The mom did well by verbally pushing in a nice way and then letting the conversation stop after her daughter asked her a second time. Bringing topics up respectfully and ending them after a few minutes can be challenging; however, it keeps parents and kids in touch with each other.

Other teenagers may quickly become comfortable with personal discussions, and parents need to respond in kind.

"So, what did you think of that movie, son, where they got into bed on their first date?"

"Mmm, I don't know."

"Oh, what do you mean?"

"Well, it just seemed so...so intense right away."

"Yeah, movies tend to do that. Get into things right away without showing the relationship building slowly."

"Dad, did you ever get into relationships quickly like that?"

"Whoa, good question, son, and I'm happy you feel comfortable to be so open with me. And I'll answer, but remember, our talks stay within the family, right?"

"Yeah, I know, Dad. Why, are you embarrassed?"

"Yes, because there was a relationship I had in college where I think we got involved too quickly."

"With Mom?"

"No, it was my freshman year, and although we didn't have sex or anything, the first night we met we were kissing heavy."

"Really? Like at a party or something?"

"Yeah, it was out at a park and there were kegs of beer and everybody was friendly."

"Mmmm."

"But I felt bad the next day because when I saw her in class, we both avoided making eye contact."

"Did you go out again?"

"No, we never did. Later we were able to say 'hi' to each other, but it was always a little uncomfortable."

"Is that how it started with you and Mom?"

"No, we started kind of slow. We were both juniors and knew we kind of liked each other, so we did things together for a couple of weeks even before our first kiss."

"How did you know you both liked each other?"

"Oh, you know what it's like when a girl likes you and you kind of feel the same shyness toward her."

"Yeah, kind of."

"Tell me what it's like for you when you like a girl?"

"Well, we just talk and stuff, but I haven't really kissed a girl yet."

"Oh, well, is that okay or do your friends tease you about it?"

"No, they don't even know; besides, they probably haven't either."

"What grade will that kind of kissing start for you and your friends?"

"I don't know, maybe this year."

"Really? How do you feel about that?"

"Well, kind of nervous, but I don't really have a girlfriend right now."

"Oh. Will you talk openly about it with her, or do you think it will kind of just happen?"

"I don't know. Probably just happen."

"It can go both ways, so I hope it's right and comfortable for both of you."

"Yeah, we'll see."

"Son, you're great to talk to; you have a nice way of talking about personal stuff."

"Hey, thanks, Dad; so do you."

Some kids will speak this openly and it is very important for the parent to stay with the topic. Getting uncomfortable and ending the conversation is not a viable option for parents wanting to raise well-prepared kids. If a parent is uncomfortable with the topic, continued practice in role-plays with a partner or trusted friend can significantly improve comfort levels.

Teenagers can and will be rebellious. This attitude underscores the importance of completely listening and asking further questions prior to eventually sharing your own opinions in a non-condescending and neutral way.

"How did you feel, John, that Tom and Amy got asked to leave the dance floor for kissing?"

"It was stupid. Everybody does it. They just did it in front of everyone."

"Oh, were they mad too?"

"Yes, everyone thought it was stupid."

"How do you think it should have been handled?"

"I don't know, but if everyone is dancing and doesn't really notice it, then leave them alone."

"When people did begin to notice, how do you think it should have been handled?"

"Say something to them first. Kind of a warning thing before telling them to leave."

"Do you think a respectful warning would have been enough for Tom and Amy?"

"Probably not, but at least they would have had a chance. These teachers always jump on us kids the first time we do something."

"Has that happened to you, too?"

"Well, yeah. Once in the hallway we were all throwing a nerf ball and four of us got I.S.S."

"I didn't know you got I.S.S."

"Yeah, well, it was for throwing a nerf ball around and it was stupid."

"So with you, too, a warning first may have been better."

"Yeah, give us a chance."

"John, have you ever been asked to leave the dance floor?"

"No, I'm not like that."

"Have you kissed your girlfriends before?"

"Dad…"

"I know, you don't have to say. I was just thinking about you and your girlfriends."

"Well, yeah, I have, but nothing heavy, and besides, I don't even have a girlfriend right now."

"Ahh, just having fun with the whole group now, huh?"

"Kind of, I guess. But I do like this one girl and she's even been talkative with me lately."

"Oh, that's great. What's her name?"

"Don't tell anyone, because it's nothing official yet.

"Okay."

"Carrie."

"Well, good for you, son. I hope it goes well for you."

"Yeah, we're in science and lunch together so it's pretty easy to talk every day."

"Well, if ever you need a ride to the mall or the movie theater with your friends to meet her and her friends, I'd be glad to drive."

"Thanks, Dad. I take it that means no single dating yet?"

"Yeah, but when you turn 16, then we can talk about that happening."

"Unfair."

"I know, but you'll be sixteen soon, and we can talk about it then. Besides, we've got to get you signed up for driver's education yet."

"Yeah, I was thinking about taking it over the summer with Rick and Joe."

"Sounds good."

The conversation flowed from the son being angry over a dance floor situation, to talking about his own possible girlfriend, to dating guidelines, to driver's education—all important and significant topics to a teenager and all listened to and handled non-judgmentally by the father. His listening and asking-questions approach without getting stuck on one subject encouraged the son to talk more, and a real closeness was forming between the father and his son. Any issue that the father felt concerned about or that needed more discussion could be brought up in a later talk. Most issues or topics that come up with teenagers do not need to be resolved or completely clarified when they initially arise.

Spread out important topics over time and keep the aspect of openness active and alive, even if it puts certain issues off until the next day or a later discussion.

False—Boys need sex and it's the girl's responsibility to say when or no. (Boys will be boys and being sexually active is cool. Girls need to use birth control, slow sex down, and are sluts if sexually active.)

Although there has been some change in this attitude over the years, boys are still generally viewed as the sexual seeker and girls as the hesitant sexual engager. Until boys and girls are seen as people first and humans with sexual differences second, such one-sided attitudes and narrowmindedness will exist. In our heads, we all know boys and girls are people first, but until we actively speak about them as people with the same potentials, positive change is thwarted. To primarily view girls and boys as different sexually, with different roles, is to create barriers and a "one is better than the other" competition. It also creates offenders and victims as each sex is primarily concerned with expressing and making itself known, recognized and accepted.

The change to this negatively sexualized view of girls and boys is in the control and powerful influence of parents. It is in the grasp of parents who talk openly about sex education and sexuality, who respectfully and age-appropriately change clothes without doors closed, and who confidently speak out against sexist and provocatively sexualized movies and television shows. To talk about the physical, sexual body parts in caring ways dissipates it's potentially negative power. To act by actually changing clothes openly within the family keeps bodily differences open and normal without hidden power, and keeps the relationship focus on the person first, and their bodily differences second. And to take a stand within the family, or publicly, against one-sided sexist events or movies demonstrates a strength in the presence of kids that is greater than the media's.

It is appropriate and healthy for kids to hear their parents make fun of disc jockeys who speak sexually to a primarily young audience, or to mock and laugh at a movie character trying to be sexually cool, or to confidently state, without shame or embarrassment in their voice, how shallow and ridiculously selfish a publisher is of pornography.

It convinces kids that their parents are bigger, stronger, and smarter than those who deal with sex offensively and incompletely. It inspires confidence and calmness in kids when they experience their own parents dealing with all aspects of sexuality without shyness and discomfort. It also creates a foundation of strength in kids who witness their parents being able to discuss any sexuality topic, and who also bring up sex questions and sexuality issues regularly.

False—An unclothed body means something sexual.

The biggest natural state that our society has taken and turned into something provocatively sexual is the unclothed human body. Because our society has given way to the media to use the human body in provocative poses to sell their product, we, as a culture, have accepted the unclothed body as a norm for meaning sex. However, it is only a norm because we, as a society, have kept our bodies covered, laughed at any kind of nudity, and have allowed the media to dictate how sex should look. By relinquishing our parental responsibility for teaching healthy sexuality over to the media and waiting until our children ask about sex, we have effectively placed ourselves and our children in a one-down position. We may not agree with the media, but until we as parents can comfortably change clothes with doors open and keep healthy sexuality picture books out on the living room table, the media-formed norms will never improve.

Until parents accept and openly deal with family nudity in comfortable ways, children and teenagers will never understand and learn that the unclothed human body can be non-sexual. The forces in our society's media are too powerful and influencing for kids to know that there is a difference without parental action. The unclothed body is naturally used to intimately express and receive love within a committed relationship; however, that is only one of its important purposes. The human body is used for many things, including movement, dance or exercise, beauty in art, strength, flexibility, warmth, nurturing children, comforting someone in pain, and friendship hugs and affection.

False—Casual sex with a friend or a one-night encounter is okay as long as it is mutual.

Intimate sex is too personal and too emotionally bonding as a human act to naively believe that it does not deeply affect the two involved. Even if an individual can justify or rationalize casual sex in their heads, they cannot program their senses to receive the experience in a muted form. The human senses of sight, sound, smell, and touch completely take in the experience at a non-verbal level, and without an ongoing, caring and committed relationship, the human spirit is prone to retreating and forming a generalized numbness to an active emotional life. These normal and unconscious reactions to intimate sex, without a deep relationship, lead to self-centeredness, low-grade depression, and a feeling of emptiness. Over time, these reactions to uncommitted intimacy erode into an energetic and active disposition for life.

False—Ignoring the sexually provocative media by becoming used to it or callused guards against taking in negative sexual messages.

Through our senses, our brains receive sexually provocative messages on several levels. Sight and hearing are the two that receive the most from radio, television, and videos. Whether it's provocative music combined with provocative scenes or the media's use of contradiction by using seemingly nice dialogue combined with provocative background music, our senses are constantly receiving. As humans, we may be capable of tuning out one of our senses, but rarely can we tune out both at the same time. Even if an individual is reading the newspaper with the television or radio on, provocative sexual messages are stored in our brains and reacted upon later. Although this effect can be small in any given moment, over prolonged periods of time, and when combined in conversation with others who hold similar one-sided beliefs, it becomes increasingly difficult to change and accept new and healthier attitudes.

This negative effect is cumulative over years of habitually listening to the radio or watching television. In our society, one cannot escape the powerful and repeated sexualized messages being played out on television and radio. We need and use television and radio to be currently connected to our world, so not watching or listening is an unrealistic option. The answer lies in limited television and radio time, but more importantly in the parental and family openness and dialogue regarding complete and healthy sexuality communication. This openness can begin slowly, but when addressed frequently over the years, its positive effect is noticeable in more mature kids as well as a developed ability to keep the media in appropriate perspective.

All of these false assumptions weigh on our minds and attitudes in subtle and destructive ways. Without showing kids that there is a difference, by openly communicating in respectfully complete dialogue on sexuality it keeps them imprisoned and unaware of the media's negative ways.

Empowering the Media or the Family?

Things that empower the media:
- Leaving the television on just for background noise.
- Laughing at sexual innuendoes while watching television without explaining them to children and teenagers.
- Self-conscious modesty due to not looking like a popular model.
- Parents not frequently bringing up sexuality questions and topics (always or usually waiting for kids to bring up sex questions).
- Making family sexuality talks long, boring (without fun emotions) and turning them into a lecture.
- Allowing unlimited television, video games, or movie time.
- Not having respectful and completely open picture books of the human body of all ages and sizes.
- Hero worship, which involves talking about longingly, or looking up to only the people one sees on television or the movies.
- Planning most evenings around the television, with kids, food, and trying to get the best seat.
- Sitting back and letting kids learn teamwork, sex education, or history from video rentals.

Things That Empower the Family:

- Having no television on at least one day a week.
- Playing a game with children that involves picking your favorite advertisement, least favorite, and why.

- Having available on the living room table books showing respectful, non-sexualized pictures of unclothed people of all ages and sizes.
- For teenagers, having available caring and respectful picture books on human intimacy.
- Making fun of a television, movie, or radio character who think they're cool because they act sexy.
- Casual family use of the bathroom and changing of clothes with doors open.
- Finding and talking about local heroes and what they did for someone else.
- Becoming involved in real-life activities like volunteering at a women's shelter, meals on wheels, or a mentoring program.
- Talking about grandparents and aunts and uncles frequently, with stories about what they do, or used to do, and what the family has learned from their wisdom and life experiences.

Importance of Father/Son Relationship

The significance of the father/son connection has not been given proper importance in our modern society. Although there are exceptions, generally a boy cannot gain true inner strength and emotional maturity without an open and close relationship with his father. An open relationship includes outside activities such as physical exercise, mental endeavors such as playing a musical instrument or reading the same book and frequent attention to inner connections such as personal talks and caring affections.

These inner connections are a challenge for any father because once our boys become teenagers, our society does not encourage such closeness. In fact, our society teaches the opposite. Instead of supporting ongoing close relationships and affection between fathers and sons, our society negates them by placing too much emphasis on the realm of sports.

In my work with teenagers, I have discovered that boys who do not receive affection and emotional support from their fathers have a tendency to overly direct those needs onto their girlfriends or mothers. This tendency is formed in our society's attitudes of men don't touch men, boys don't cry, and males hug females, not other males.

Often, while with their girlfriends, these type of boys act like puppies, starving for affection. However, their overly touchy demeanor quickly changes to hurt or anger if her affections slow down or she wants to go out with her friends. With their mothers, these boys tend to either show off in an attempt for praise or expect to be catered to. They are usually demanding and almost always verbally disrespectful. These behavior patterns occur because these boys are attempting to meet their normal affectionate needs through society's only accepted way: with females. Therefore, a boy will never be internally fulfilled because he needs a balance of female and male affection in order to remain emotionally calm and not become aggressive. In his lack of nurturance from his father, and his partial satisfaction at being touched by his girlfriend, he remains blind to his whole self. Over time, this condition often leads young men into depression, or worse, into becoming physically intimidating to get what they want within their personal relationships. At a talk in Minneapolis, Chris Ringer, a therapist, offered an axiom for this condition. "Show me a man who hits his wife, and I'll show you a man who misses his father."

Usually, with boys this natural drive for a father's—as well as a moth-er's—affection is disguised and manipulated in their puppy looks and girlfriend dependency, rather than physical intimidation which tends to occur as they get older. However, their hurt and potential anger is just beneath their needy demeanor. Teenage boys do not do this because they are going through a phase. They are blindly doing it with their girlfriends because internally they long for it from an unconnected father or other men in their lives. Fathers who do not attend to this inner side of parenting a son are leaving them with a legacy of need, mixed with hurt and anger, which renders them emotionally anxious and overly controlling in their female relationships. If personal talks, including sexuality and sex education, and comfortable affection and play are not experienced by sons from their fathers, they are left lost in the superficiality of sports scores, all-star wrestling, racecars, and unfortunately, unstable girlfriend relationships.

Because of their common gender and makeup, it is a father's absolute responsibility and obligation to provide well-rounded parenting, personal talks—including sexuality, and frequently giving comfortable, affectionate experiences to their sons. Without both, our sons will and do falter. I believe domestic violence and the pornographic industry exists and is expanding because it is replete with men who miss their fathers. Emotionally, these young men need a father or masculine nurturance and it is only a father or other men who can give it. As modern day fathers, we need to accept the challenge of complete and well-rounded parenting, not only for the sake of our son's appropriate emotional growth, but also to make certain negative behavior toward women does not occur in another generation of young men.

Genuinely Protecting Children's Innocence

Often parents will state that they don't want to tell their kids about sex education too soon. They want them to be free of the world's issues and complexities as long as possible. Although it is imperative to protect children by maintaining safe limits and healthy play, it is extremely important to view the world through their eyes. To see what they see. This also includes hearing what they hear. We cannot just look at them and see their innocence and beauty. We have to frequently get on their level and take in and try to understand what they receive everyday. This level viewing with our young children allows us to monitor, protect, and guide what their world reveals to them.

If our kindergarteners, 1st, and 2nd graders watch television, hear popular music on the radio, witness or hear older children talk, or dine at fast food restaurants, they are exposed to numerous sexual messages each day. Young children will ignore most of what they don't understand; however, they do retain some of the provocative and double-meaning sexual messages that naturally evoke an emotional response. To hope they will just forget or ignore what continually hits their senses everyday is a fantasy. Living in our media-saturated society, they will not forget. On the contrary, sexual messages get reinforced every day. Over months and years, these daily—or even weekly—subtle sexual messages become ingrained and grow into a significant aspect of one's attitudes.

There is something parents can do to protect their children's innocence. In very simple and caring ways, parents can teach their young children about human bodies, respectful sexual words, and eventually how babies are created prior to their immersion in our world. It can begin slowly by taking baths with toddlers, to changing clothes with doors open, to looking at picture books of human bodies with

1st graders, to sharing the miracle of love and birth with 2nd graders. These experiences and talks can be done slowly throughout their young years, and they can be done in short, comfortably flowing moments. It is not necessary to make the talks long and involved, but merely acknowledging and easy. Children's interest and respect will occur in the same way as it is addressed and enacted by their parents.

If our young children are exposed to human bodies in a comfortable way and also respectful sexuality talk before frequent exposure to the media, they can retain their innocence and love of life. This kind of family openness and respect creates a very caring and supportive environment which gives children a solid foundation for growth and keeps the media in perspective. In reality, by bringing the very aspects of human bodies and caring sexuality knowledge to our children first, we are protecting and prolonging their innocence. This approach makes all the difference in a child's world and it is one of the early and meaningful gifts that parents can give to their children.

Like Father, Like Son

One of the more important developmental steps a young boy has to achieve is appropriate identification with his father. Young boys encounter different levels of this stage at various ages. Grade school boys usually over-exaggerate their fathers into heroes. Middle school boys continue to exaggerate their father's positive qualities, but when angry, they can also say extremely negative comments. High school boys have a tendency to balance their father's behaviors and influence while continuing to need his consistent presence. When boys witness their father, at any age, act inappropriately or in a sexual manner toward women, they will be deeply affected. Often boys will imitate and uphold their father's opinions and behaviors. Other boys will store situations in their memory to be acted upon later. Some boys will be confused or unsure of themselves when relating to the opposite sex.

In order to pass on a respectful and comfortable outlook and attitude toward the opposite sex, fathers need to relate to women as equals—not as someone to be cool in front of, or to dominate with knowledge or strength, or to laugh at, but someone to talk with as an equal. Our society is filled with sexual messages that stereotype and label women, and which confuse and mislead young boys. Therefore, it is imperative for fathers to go beyond the norm and frequently demonstrate to their sons equality in relating to the opposite sex. When sons are close to their fathers, verbally and affectionately, they develop a strong core personality as well as a natural comfort with same-sex and opposite-sex friends. Boys who are not close to their fathers are at a disadvantage and often fall behind in social skills when compared to their same-age counterparts.

Whatever captures a father's attention will also hold a son's attention. If a father primarily views women as sexual objects by looking at pornographic material, then the son will most likely begin to view woman similarly. If a father speaks respectfully and has friends who are women, then the son will likely view women as people and treat them with equality. A father's role in his son's developing male identity and how he relates to the opposite sex cannot be underscored enough. A son's view of the females in his world and engaging successfully in relationships with them is significantly predicated on a positive relationship with his father and on how his father relates to women in his life.

3.) Reminders for Fathers and Mothers, Axioms, and Comments

Reminder for Fathers of Sons
Spend time with my son in various activities and sports.
Include quiet times of reading or listening to music. Hear
him out when he's upset, allow him to have tears, and
touch him—in fun as well as supportively. Make hugs
frequent at any age and tell him I'm proud when he helps
another.

A Mother's Other Calling

A young man's sexual maturity would not be complete without the involvement and influence of his mother. Generally, a boy's first dependence is on his mother. As boys get older, they often try to break away or balance their mother/son relationship through anger, cynicism, or rebellion against her authority. A mother's responsibility is to guide this natural balancing by her son in a respectful and adult-monitored way. This equates to allowing a son to slowly pull away from your opinions, yet always be free to come back to your closeness and caring. Sons need to always feel their mother's support, while at the same time feeling supported when seeking periods of independence. The position a mother takes with her son is having one arm around his shoulder while the other is laid open and gesturing out to the world around him. Allowing him to comfortably lean on either arm at different times, guilt-free, is exceptional parenting a mother can give to her son.

In practical terms, this breaks down into several steps. One is when a boy is pre-school age, allowing him to ride his bike around the block and being in the yard to hug him when he returns. Another step is during the grade school years. When a boy rebels and does not want to take his turn at doing the dishes, his mother is there to calmly (and not personally defending herself and her reasoning) make his choice clear of either complying or getting a consequence. No amount of his verbal disrespect or physical attempts at intimidation sways the responsible and respectful mother. She maintains her calm and steadfast mood, knowing that the situation is his problem, not hers. It is her responsibility to allow him his verbal or behavioral gyrations in his attempt to work it out for himself. She is the constant; he is the jumpy one. Sometimes these situations resolve quickly and other times a mother needs to hold her mood and solid position for an hour while her son slowly figures out what is best.

Another step is when boys are preteen and young teenagers. A strong mother will hold to her expectations and allow her son to choose and act within her guidelines. Whether it's choosing between an hour of television a day, two hours with friends, or exercise each day, the framework is set. The son makes choices within guidelines, without his mother doing it for him.

Another level of responsible mother/son parenting is during his teenage years. Allowances for more privileges and independence are given step-bystep, and respecting his privacy with friends is essential. Affection needs to continue throughout these years and should be given in a comfortable mother and son manner, not in joking with girlfriend or boyfriend undertones to it.

Overall, a mother's appropriate and respectful parenting corresponds directly to his needs and responsibilities. Consistent privileges, consequences, allowing him to get upset while you calmly watch him choose, and ongoing affection all provide him with the basics for growing into a well-liked, and balanced young man. When a son's connection with his mother has always been close with adequate room for independence without guilt, a son grows to not only respect women, but also to uphold them equally in his male and female relationships.

A Reminder for Mothers of Sons
Trust and use my experience to compliment him when he's
respectful, and confront and give him a consequence when
he is inappropriate. Listen to him in times of need, and
always return his smile. Let him know when I am proud
and give equal support for his giving side as much as for
his sports. Use my steady, calm strength when he tries to
intimidate, and always hug him with my head above his.

A Father's Other Responsibility

A father owes it to his daughter to look at and view a woman as an individual person, and not as a sexual possibility. If a father does not hold a person-first attitude toward women, then he cannot truly be close to his daughter, because seeing women as even distant sexual possibilities means closeness with the opposite sex equates to sex. A father cannot be sexual with his daughter, so if his worldview is one of seeing woman as sexual beings first, that attitude impedes true closeness with his daughter.

However, a father who is just sexual with the person he is romantically in love with, and who views all other people as individuals, can very comfortably hug, talk, and be close to his daughter at any age. The talks and affections he shares with his daughter are so appropriate and natural in the well-adjusted father that his daughter grows and develops in an emotionally healthy way. She tends to carry herself confidently and independently, whether she is in the company of girls or boys. For a daughter to have at least one relationship with a male in her life where her sex is not reacted to allows her immense freedom to be herself. This, in an unconscious way, guides her in keeping sexuality in perspective within her boyfriend relationships. She can truly understand and recognize when her boyfriend is basing his relationship with her on sex and personal gain, or when it is focused on the truer aspects of herself as a person first and an equal partner in the relationship.

Fathers who naturally treat other people as individuals first and who do not see women in terms of a remote sexual possibility are a step ahead of other men who have been steeped in our society's view of women. Men who have not confronted our society's male and female roles are at a disadvantage. Although these men and fathers do not necessarily view their daughters in a sexual way, sometimes, due to being raised with a one-sided viewpoint of women and sex, these men simply and unknowingly tend to avoid initiating affection with their daughters, or even recoil when the daughter is affectionate toward them. Fathers who find themselves in this limiting and often times uncomfortable situation can take an active role in changing their one-sided sexual mindset. This unsexualization process begins by limiting television viewing time, reading books recommended by women, taking an active stand against the provocative depictions of women in our society, frequently perusing magazines and picture books that depict the unclothed human body in non-sexual ways with a spouse, discussing sexuality and sex education issues with other male friends, and volunteering time at a women's shelter.

A father who finds himself in a situation where he rarely—or no longer—is affectionate with his teenage daughter can and ought to make the personal changes necessary in order to provide two significant relationship aspects for his daughter. One, the unsexualizing of the majority of male and female relationships; and two, the equalizing of the sexes and their roles in our society. Although these re-educating activities may sound unusual, it is only a father's discomfort with sexuality and his inner competition with women that hold him back from the positive, personal change that can greatly benefit his daughter. The natural and unbiased affection that a father shares with his daughter is invaluable for her becoming a confident and strong young woman.

> *A Reminder for Fathers of Daughters*
> *Listen to my daughter when she talks, without trying to fix her issues for her. Respect her when she's upset and angry by not leaving the conversation. Give her the chance and time to learn from mistakes in her own way. Allow her to fix things, show her how to change the oil in the car, and always unselfishly support her dreams and endeavors. If she experiences these things from me, she will expect them from other men and in her personal relationships.*

A Mother and her Daughter

For a mother to impart confidence in her daughter's decisions, strength in her voice, and holding to her intuitions even in the face of opposition is to give her the tools for success. Our society is fast-paced and complex, and for a young woman to keep our sexualized culture in perspective and have the acumen to succeed, daughters need the deep strength and wisdom of their mother and all women. These traits can only be passed on through a close and unselfish relationship with the women in her life. Sometimes this may involve a daughter staying up late and getting a chance to just listen to her mother, aunts, and grandma conversing into the night. Other times it may involve shopping for bras, clothes, and tampons with just her mother, then taking time to have lunch together. Other times it may involve taking a trip to look at colleges, along with a close friend and her mother. Volunteer work at a hospital or coaching a team are also excellent growth experiences. Attending a peaceful march for women's rights or a camping trip with her girlfriends can be very beneficial life experiences.

When these activities are done in the company of other girls and women, a daughter has the chance to slowly develop her own identity and her personality. When experienced consistently throughout her growing years, a daughter is given an opportunity for stability and strength that carries her through many life experiences and relationships.

A Reminder for Mothers of Daughters
Support her independence and let her voice raise. Allow her to choose above my expectations and show her that coming into womanhood is special and strong. Give her the wisdom that I share with all women, and let her witness me talking to my partner with confidence and equality. Hear her dreams and let her go so that I can truly and unselfishly be close to her throughout our lives.

Keeping Sports in Perspective

Although subtle, an over-involvement in sports is a significant aspect of the negatively sexualized grooming process that is primarily occurring with our young boys. The key to keeping sports activities in perspective is remembering that it is lower-level learning. It is a group of individuals coming together, usually for fun, and acting cooperatively in order to beat another group. It can be fun and interesting because it is unpredictable and exhilarating to try hard in hopes of winning, coupled with the chance of losing being ever-present. However, it can also turn serious and rageful as competitors actually hurt each other in their drive for winning at any cost. This sometimes rageful intensity is increased by parents yelling at their children, a coach wanting a championship more than anything, and large amounts of money going to the players in professional sports.

With kids, they generally learn team cooperation, obtain physical exercise, and meet new friends, all in fun. Problems arise when too much energy and family scheduling focus on a child's sports events. This creates a pattern of priority which gives kids the message that sports and their performance are more important than family activities. Giving this level of priority to a child's sports events slowly erodes the motivation and the importance for life's other relationships. Often a more "laid-back" or "come-to-me" type of attitude is common among kids who have too much focus on their sports.

On the other hand, teamwork in order to help others is high-level learning. The purpose of coming together, cooperatively, to help others is a process that actually benefits both groups. Examples include a group of students traveling into their cities to build homes with Habitat for Humanity; taking a bus to another state to help flood or tornado victims, or volunteering on a field trip for children at a women's shelter. This type of high-level learning activities teach cooperation in a deep and personal way, give both groups a positive feeling, and provide strong and enduring memories of new relationships.

Balance, a variety of experiences, and working together for the benefit of another group of people ought to be an integral part of our children's growing years. If our kids experience numerous activities including high-level learning, their well-rounded growth and road to maturity is intact. If our kids experience only a few activities or focus primarily on one sport, which is low-level learning, they lose precious real life and relationship practice experiences that all kids need for success in the adult world. Involvement in sports is appropriate and fun if kept in perspective and as a secondary priority to the personally enhancing, high-level learning activities. When kids are well-rounded, from frequently prioritized high-level as opposed to low-level learning experiences, the openness and respect for appropriate sexuality talks and experiences are a natural and comfortably accepted part of growing up.

4.) *Closure*

The possibilities for parenting children and teenagers through our sexualized society are concrete, respectfully reality-based, and an enhancement of their personal strength. They are also necessary if we expect our kids to grow into knowledgeable children, mature teenagers, and successful adults. The overriding themes of openness, frequent talks, and respectful experiences in the area of sexuality can carry our kids into the higher echelons of personal relationships and individual independence. There will be doubters of this open sexuality approach, but more often than not it is because they do not have the personal confidence or strength to resolve their own sexual discomforts. They tend to rationalize their rigid or un-open attitude toward sexuality by citing religious or moral beliefs, because for them their defensive words keep the whole uncomfortable topic at a distance.

In our society, there are also other individuals who tout the openness of sexuality to anyone who will listen. In their drive to compensate for lost relationships or past discomforts, they have extended themselves too far into the realm of "Anything goes," or "Let's all be open with everybody." This extreme position is also inappropriate because it spreads oneself too thin, and therefore prevents relationships from growing gradually in privacy, trust, and strength.

The most optimal position for parents to uphold is to avoid these extremes and discover a comfortable and appropriate openness level within their own families. An individual family's comfortably paced approach insures stability and attentive nurturance for one's own children and teenagers. Branching out in order to share with others is secondary to one's own family's security and growth. When kids learn and re-learn, and experience and re-experience openness and respectful experiences within their own families, their personality roots become increasingly stronger and opening up to others occurs naturally. Their speed and ability to keep pace with those around them will only happen after they've gained strength, respect, and appropriate caring within their own families. A well-balanced, appropriately paced, and completely open approach to parenting children and teenagers affords them the chance for clear thinking and personal success.

A healthy sexual society is one that can deal openly and respectfully with all aspects of sexuality. It recognizes that there is a difference between an unclothed body and sex. It embraces and honors the sexual maturation of its adolescents, and it is a society that can talk beyond the media, answer all of the sexual questions of its children, and illuminate all of the sexual curiosities of its teenagers. These values need to be experienced first and foremost within the family. Future success for our kids in the area of personal strength and relationship intimacy is entirely dependent on how well parents respectfully open up and present the whole topic of sexuality.

The more children experience unclothed bodies at a young age within the caring and respectful atmosphere of their home, the more likely they will see others as people first. The more teenagers experience frequent openness to all their sexual questions and curiosities, the more likely they will see sex as a choice and responsibility, not a given. And the more children and teenagers experience this caring and respectful openness and comfort with sexuality within their families, the more mature they become.

The current status quo does not work for our children and teenagers, and therefore it is a parent's responsibility and purpose to embrace this new and open way to raise their kids. With this new, open approach parents can make a positive and long-lasting difference for their children and teenagers. To parent beyond the media in a caring and respectful way is a very powerful and deeply impacting way to raise kids. When these values and open experiences are passed on to our children and teenagers, then truly, we have kids we can be proud of in the knowledge that we contributed to the most significant part of their growing years.

Organizations that Support and Promote Respectful and Healthy Sexuality Education

S.I.E.C.U.S. (Sexuality Information and Education Council of the United States)
130 West 42nd Street, #350
New York, NY 10036-7802
1-212-819-9770

Carnegie Council on Adolescent Development
P.O. Box 753
Waldorf, MD 20604
1-202-429-7979

The Kinsey Institute
175 Fifth Avenue
New York, NY 10010
1-800-221-7945

The Henry J. Kaiser Family Foundation
2400 Sand Hill Road
Menlo Park, CA 94025
1-800-656-4533

The Alan Guttmacher Institute
120 Wall Street, 21st Floor
New York, NY 10005
1-212-248-1111

Centers for Disease Control and Prevention
1600 Clifton Road N.E.
Atlanta, GA 30333
1-800-311-3435

Planned Parenthood Federation of America
810 Seventh Avenue
New York, NY
1-800-829-PPFA

National Coalition to Support Sexuality Education (developed by S.I.E.C.U.S.)
Public Policy Office, Suite 206
1711 Connecticut Ave. N.W.
Washington, D.C. 20009
1-202-265-2405

Family Health Council, Inc.
960 Pennsylvania Ave., #600
Pittsburgh, PA 15222
1-412-288-0518

Advocates for Youth
1025 Vermont Ave. N.W. #200
Washington, D.C. 20005
1-202-347-5700

F.L.A.S.H. (Family Life and Sexual Health), Sex Education Curricula
Seattle-King County Dept. of Public Health
Health Education Material Sales
400 Yesler Way, 3rd Floor
Seattle, WA 98104
1-206-296-4902

Girls Incorporated National Resource Center
441 West Michigan Street
Indianapolis, IN 46202
1-317-634-7546

Project SNAPP: Skills and knowledge for AIDS and pregnancy prevention for the Middle Grades
E.T.R. Associates
P.O. Box 1830
Santa Cruz, CA 95061
1-800-321-4407

Endnotes

1. Kilbourne, Jean, *Deadly Persuasion: Why Women and Girls Must Fight the Addictive Power of Advertising.* N.Y. Free Press, 1999.

2. Pirsig, Robert. *Zen and the Art of Motorcycle Maintenance.* N.Y. Bantam Books, 1973.

3. Kirby, D. "Sexuality and HIV Education Programs in Schools," In Kirby (Ed), *Sex Education in the Schools.* Menlo Park, CA, Kaiser Family Foundation, 1994. pp. 1-41

4. Piaget, Jean. *Six Psychological Studies.* N.Y. Random House, 1968, p. 20.

5. Erickson, Erik. . *Childhood and Society.* N.Y. W.W. Norton & Company, 1950, pp. 252-258.

6. Erickson, Erik. *Childhood and Society.* N.Y. W.W. Norton & Company, 1950, p. 262.

7. Ansuini, C. and Woite, J. & R. "The Source, Accuracy, and Impact of Initial Sexuality Information on Lifetime Wellness." *Adolescence,* Sum 1996, V 31, p. 283.

8. Chernin, Kim. *The Obsession: Reflections on the Tyranny of Slenderness.* Harper Collins, N.Y. 1981.

9. "Everything You Wanted to Know about Sex." *Time,* 15 June 1998.

10. Beaty, Lee. "Effects of Paternal Absence on Male Adolescents' Peer Relations and Self-image." *Adolescence,* 1995, Vol. 30, No. 120, pp. 873-880.

11. Blankenhorn, David. *Fatherless America Confronting Our Most Urgent Social Problem*. N.Y. Basic Books: Harper Collins, 1995.

12. Biller, H.B., Bauhm, R.M. "Father Absence Perceived Maternal Behavior, and Masculinity of Self-concept Among Junior High Boys." *Developmental Psychology*, 1971, Vol. 4, No. 2, pp. 178-181.
Bushweller, K. "Turning Our Backs on Our Boys." *The American School Board Journal*, 1994, Vol. 181, pp. 20-25.
D'Angelo, L. Weinberger, D. & Feldman, S. "Like Father, Like Son? Predicting Male Adolescents Adjustment from Parents Distress and Self-restraint." *Developmental Psychology*, 1995, Vol. 31, No. 6, pp. 883-96.

13. Lamb, Michael E. *The Role of the Father in Child Development*. N.Y. J. Wiley & Sons, Inc., 1997, p 154.

14. Haapasalo, J. & Tremblay, R.E. "Physically Aggressive Boys From Ages 6 to 12: Family Background, Parenting Behavior, and Prediction of Delinquency." *Journal of Consulting and Clinical Psychology*, 1994, Vol. 62, pp. 1044-1052.

15. Amato, P. "Father Involvement and Self-Esteem of Children and Adolescents." *Australian Journal of Sex, Marriage, and Family*, 1986, Vol. 7, pp. 6-16.

16. National Center for Health Statistics, *National Vital Statistics Report*, Vol. 47, no. 9.

17. (1) Kirby, D. "School-Based Programs to Reduce Sexual Risk Behaviors: A review of effectiveness," *Public Health Reports*, May-June, 1994, vol. 109, no. 3, pp. 339-60.
(2) National Guidelines Task Force, *Guidelines for Comprehensive Sexuality Education, K-12th Grade*, New York: Sex Information and Education Council of the Unites States, 1991.
(3) A. Grunseit and S. Kippax, "Effects of Sex Education on Young People's Behaviour," *World Health Organization*, 1994.

About the Author

J.E. Wright, M.A., L.I.C.S.W.

Mr. Wright has been a therapist for 27 years, having obtained his undergraduate degree in psychology and completed his graduate work in social service administration at the University of Chicago. He has worked with over 3,000 children and teenagers and their families. He has written articles for Social Work journals, Practice Digest, and the Minnesota Police Chief's magazine. He is a foster parent trainer and a workshop leader on topics ranging from self-esteem, child sexual abuse recovery, and parenting adolescents. His professional expertise is in the clinical work with children and teenagers using therapeutic play, sandtray therapy, and work with their families.

Mr. Wright may be contacted at 952-431-2191 for workshops, training, or consultations.